CAI

SOURCEBOOK

ROBERT L. BURKE

Prentice-Hall, Inc. Englewood Cliffs, New Jersey 07632

Library of Congress Cataloging in Publication Data

Burke, Robert L.
  CAI sourcebook.

  Includes index.
  1. Computer-assisted instruction. I. Title.
  LB1028.5.B873   371.3'9445   81-15356
  ISBN 0-13-110155-2   AACR2

Jacket Design by R. D. Graphics/Richard Ross

Printed in the United States of America

10 9 8 7 6 5 4 3 2 1

Prentice-Hall International, Inc., *London*
Prentice-Hall of Australia Pty. Limited, *Sydney*
Prentice-Hall of Canada, Ltd., *Toronto*
Prentice-Hall of India Private Limited, *New Delhi*
Prentice-Hall of Japan, Inc., *Tokyo*
Prentice-Hall of Southeast Asia Pte. Ltd., *Singapore*
Whitehall Books Limited, *Wellington, New Zealand*

CONTENTS

Chapter 6
CAI FRAME PROTOCOLS

Chapter 7
CAI LESSON DESIGNS

Chapter 8
VALIDATION OF CAI LESSONS

A GLOSSARY OF CAI TERMS

INDEX

PREFACE

The microcomputer is an incredibly powerful tool for learning. While the microcomputer bears a functional relationship to large, predecessor computers, it did not evolve from them in the usual sense of evolution. Rather, the microcomputer represents a large jump, particularly in cost reduction. These powerful but inexpensive microcomputers are rapidly finding their way into the hands of large numbers of educational users — users who vary greatly in sophistication, training and experience. Many of these educational users are finding it desirable to create computer assisted instruction lessons. Most of them lack any specific training in the use of computers, or, in the development of self-instructional materials. While training in the use of computers is becoming increasingly available, there remains much more difficult to find opportunities to learn the concepts and techniques of developing self-instructional materials.

This book is intended to fill this void and enable the inservice educator to learn to produce CAI lessons. It is also intended that this book will serve as a textbook in graduate and undergraduate education courses in CAI courseware development.

The widespread and increasing use of microcomputers in schools has created a tremendous demand for instructional courseware. This state of affairs presents a great opportunity for the person who learns to create instructional courseware. Publishers and software production and distribution houses are aggressively seeking good new instructional courseware.

This book provides a step-by-step introduction to the systematic development and validation of CAI courseware. Even the veteran CAI author will find helpful material, particularly in the area of instructional writing, validation and improvement of lessons and courseware quality control.

1

BECOMING A COMPUTER ASSISTED INSTRUCTION AUTHOR

INTRODUCTION

This book is intended to fill a need for knowledge of computer assisted instruction (CAI) which has been created by the sudden availability of inexpensive, powerful, microcomputers in classrooms all across the country. The book is intended for those with little or no knowledge of instructional technology or computers.

1

The term **computer assisted instruction**, or **CAI**, as it is used here, refers to the direct use of computers, (in this case microcomputers), to provide primary instructional service.

It is anticipated that this book can be used as a sourcebook for those who would like to teach themselves to develop CAI lessons. It is further hoped that the book may serve as a text for education courses, both undergraduate and graduate, in the development of CAI lessons. Finally, it is hoped that it will serve as a reference work even for the experienced CAI author.

THE COMPUTER ASSISTED INSTRUCTION COURSEWARE SHORTAGE

At the present time, there is a critical shortage of courseware for CAI. Publishers, computer software houses, and computer manufacturers who had little or no interest in CAI as late as 1978, are now searching vigorously for CAI courseware.

The reason for this is the development of microcomputers. The introduction and rapid spread of inexpensive, powerful, reliable, and simple-to-use microcomputers has dropped the average cost per terminal hour, from several dollars per hour on each terminal of a large computer to a few cents per hour on a microcomputer. This factor has caused the number of potential CAI users to increase at an astronomical rate.

The advent and rapid acceptance of microcomputers has created a tremendous demand for computer assisted instruction courseware. Schools and training organizations are installing microcomputers in large numbers. Initial applications are varied, from word processing to teaching computer programming. However, in almost all environments there is eventually a desire to use the microcomputer for computer assisted instruction. CAI in this sense means direct instructional delivery in which the computer mediates instruction, simulating a human tutor.

This situation has created an unanticipated and unprecedented demand for CAI courseware. In fact, to a very real extent, the use of microcomputers in schools and company training rooms is limited only by the availability of CAI courseware.

The result of this is a critical need to create computer assisted instruction courseware. There is simply very little instructional courseware to run on the microcomputer. Material which was designed for large systems cannot be directly adapted, and indeed, there is little of that available either.

The other side of the coin is the shortage of CAI authors. To be sure, there are a few professional CAI authors who have experience in large-computer CAI. For the most part, they prefer to stay with what they know, large computers. In addition, since large computer CAI development was somewhat limited by the small number of users, few learning experts entered this field. There is no large pool of trained people to draw from.

There are also a few people who work in microcomputer CAI. They are primarily self-taught, drawing on natural talent and ingenuity, but are typically not in touch with considerable body of knowledge or the people involved with large-computer CAI. This book is designed, in part, to help bridge this gap, to make the wisdom accumulated by the field of large-computer CAI available in a form which is relevant to microcomputer CAI authors.

The rest of this chapter will be devoted to an examination of some of the reasons you might want to be a CAI author, and to the identification of a number of topics which you should consider. The chapter will also help you to define, as well as you can at this point, your own motives for becoming a CAI author. Once your motives are clear, you can determine what your objectives should be for your personal preparation. Finally, the chapter will help you to lay out a specific plan for becoming a CAI author.

WHY SHOULD I BECOME A CAI AUTHOR?

A psychologist friend once told me, "Nobody does anything unless he anticipates an appropriate payoff." I remember that I argued with him at the time. As the years have gone by, however, I have come to agree with the statement more and more.

A corollary of the statement may be even more true, "The more reasons one has for pursuing an endeavor, the more likely one is to persevere." Let's explore some of the reasons a person might want to go to the effort of becoming a CAI author.

To Provide Students with Optional Ways to Learn

Many of us have gone into our chosen fields for a variety of reasons — sometimes very personal reasons. I am no exception. One of the reasons I am in the field of individualized instruction is that I have witnessed the failure of traditional educational methods in the lives of people close to me. I think CAI is one of the most elegant alternatives to traditional methods we have.

Through the the use of CAI, the teacher can extend appropriate educational opportunities to a wide variety of students, including both the academically talented and those who are in academic trouble. With this electronic

3

assistance the teacher can handle a far larger range of abilities in the same class.

To Provide Personal Satisfaction

Writing CAI can be a very enjoyable activity in and of itself. This is probably the best reason and should accompany any of the others. I am reminded of an experience I once had in a seminar in writing given by a distinguished professor. It happened that he became emeritized on the very day of that seminar. He said, "I'm taking this occasion to impart something to you which I think is wisdom. The only valid reason to do anything is because you enjoy it." He added, "And now I am in the enviable position to act on that belief." Hopefully, you will find writing CAI enjoyable, and it will provide you with some of that same spirit of independence.

To Enhance One's Professional Reputation

There are still very few "experts" in the CAI field. As a result, it is still quite possible to develop a good reputation in your region or even nationally. Conventions of all kinds are very eager to hear from people with experience and expertise in CAI. It is still relatively easy to get an article or book published in this area as well.

To Make a Contribution to the Profession

Many people feel a very strong need to make a contribution to their profession — to add to the body of knowledge, to contribute to the improvement of instructional technique, and so forth. CAI authorship is an especially needed service at this time, and a body of professional knowledge is much needed as well.

To Use the Skill in One's Present Position

You may want simply to use your skills as a CAI author to benefit your own immediate students and to provide you with alternatives within your own classroom. Given the shortage of CAI courseware, which is likely to continue for quite some time, if you are interested in using CAI in your own classroom, on a comprehensive basis, you may have to write much of it yourself.

4

To Provide Additional Income

Inflation has everyone concerned about their ability to keep pace. Even a limited effort in CAI can result in the production of CAI which a publisher may accept, and which can then earn royalties for you.

To Change Careers

For the past eight years, I have directed graduate programs for in-service teachers. At least half the teachers I have known have harbored the secret desire to change careers. Often, it was to "go into industry" or to "start a business." This seems to be particularly true of teachers with at least ten years of service — a kind of "ten year itch," if you will. Becoming a competent CAI author can provide that option many people are looking for.

To Provide a Second Career After Retirement

Many teachers are able to retire while they are still quite young and healthy. They take with them a wealth of experience which is an unfortunate waste. By becoming a CAI author, the retired teacher can begin a new career which makes good use of that experience. You can get started in CAI well before you retire and experience a much smoother transition to retirement.

To Change Jobs Within the Same Career Field

In periods of decreasing enrollments, job mobility for teachers becomes very difficult and risky. Having competency as a CAI author can put you in demand and give you the mobility you desire.

To Increase Job Security

In a tight job market, a diversity of scarce and valued skills is still one of the best guaranties that you will survive cutbacks. Although there are still few jobs for full-time teachers of computer science available in the schools, there seem to be many positions for math and science teachers who have knowledge of computers. Many people expect a new area of teacher certification in computer education to be established. If that happens, and I,m quite certain that it will, there will be many jobs created for teachers of computer topics of all kinds.

To Influence Vendors Who May Give You Equipment

It is still the practice for some manufacturers to give equipment grants to professionals, such as teachers, whom they feel are capable of producing programs and applications which might favorably affect their volume of sales. Since there is such a shortage of CAI courseware, this remains a priority area for manufacturers.

To Become Self-Employed

You may not want to start your own company. You might prefer simply to become a free-lance CAI author. There are well over one hundred microcomputer-based CAI courseware distributing firms. That does not include the established publishers and microcomputer manufacturers who are now becoming involved in CAI in significant numbers. The royalties you can expect to receive are often at a higher rate than is usual for books, and the selling price is likely to be higher as well. Revisions are usually done on at least an annual basis and they will bring you good royalties as well.

Some outlets will want to buy your software outright. Depending on your circumstances, and your continuing interest in the CAI package, this could in many cases be an attractive alternative.

To Start a CAI Courseware Production and Distribution Company

It is not unrealistic to think that you might become a magnate of the "knowledge industry," a part of the "information industry" as it has come to be called. The information industry is America's leading growth industry and is predicted to remain so for at least the next two decades. Many millionaires have already been made within the information industry and no doubt many more will be. Some of the largest information industry corporations started with an idea and a few hundred dollars in capital. It is still happening and you are still in time to get your piece of the pie.

You can start as simply or as grandly as suits your circumstances. Your success will depend, in great part, upon your creativity and your energy level — these will determine the quality, appropriateness, and therefore, the acceptance of your products.

6

For the educator who has the motivation and the skill to start a company, a CAI courseware development, production and distribution company is an excellent choice at this time for a lot of reasons.

A CAI company will allow you to capitalize on professional experience you already have. You can start slowly, in stages, even before you give up your current position. In fact, you may never have to give up your present position.

It is a clean business which you can run from your own home. It is ideal for a "mom-and-pop" or family business.

There is little need for investment capital. During the development of your courseware product, your only investment is your time. You don't have to maintain large inventories. You can quickly duplicate your courseware onto cassettes or discs as orders are received, package the discs or tapes along with an information sheet or manual in a large zip-lock plastic bag and send it out. You can even print the information sheet or manual on the printer of your own computer as required.

Once your company has begun to succeed and to produce capital you can hire part-time and even full-time help, and you are on your way.

HOW DO YOU GET TO BE A CAI AUTHOR?

One of the purposes of this book is to help you clarify your goals with respect to CAI — to assess your present circumstance, and to develop a plan for becoming a CAI author. In the previous section you saw some of the possible motives for learning to write CAI. Perhaps some of yours were among them. Perhaps you found some there which you could adopt. And then, maybe you have other motives which were not there. At any rate, knowing your motives can help you to set your objectives and plan how you will attain them.

This section will help you with that process. We will cover some of the steps you may wish to take. The balance of the book will then help you attain your objective of becoming a CAI author.

Decide Which Microcomputer You Will Work With

There are several bases for deciding which microcomputer you will write for. You may not really have a choice if you only have access to one type of unit. Some school districts have "adopted" one brand of microcomputer and will not permit any others to be purchased within the district, for example.

If, however, you do have some latitude, you will want to consider such things as the popularity, reputation for serviceability, CAI authoring systems available, CAI author languages available, and general features and capabilities of the particular microcomputer. There is one microcomputer of which almost three hundred thousand units have been sold, for example. Good courseware written for this microcomputer is almost certain to find widespread utilization. Some brands have been adopted by entire states. If you happen to live in such a state, you would probably want to write for the state-adopted microcomputer.

Some microcomputers are better adapted to certain content areas than others. You would certainly want to choose a microcomputer which was well suited to the area in which you would write.

Get Some General Background Familiarity With Microcomputers

This book will deal exclusively with the hard-to-find knowledge specific to CAI authorship. Therefore, if you have no familiarity with microcomputers at all, you may want to read some basic material such as some of the many magazines and journals devoted exclusively to microcomputers. Perhaps you will want to pick up one of the many books on microcomputers which are now available. You may also find it quite worthwhile to take one of the courses in microcomputers which are becoming increasingly available through higher education institutions, inservice training, and even some computer stores.

Develop Some Background Knowledge of CAI Development Thus Far

Despite the fact that CAI has thus far not had much of an effect on education or training, there has nevertheless been a lot of effort and thought expended by those few people who have been in a position to have their work subsidized in some way. The wisdom and experience of many of these people has been recorded in a diverse set of articles and books. To collect and digest even a significant portion of this material would be a prodigious task to say the least.

Chapter 2 is a brief synopsis of some of the good ideas in this literature as well as an exploration of some of the philosophical underpinnings of the technology of CAI.

8

Choose a CAI Authoring System, CAI Language, or General Computer Language

At this time, there are basically three ways of authoring CAI, a CAI **authoring system**, a CAI **author language**, and a **general purpose computer language**. The CAI authoring system, which is a rather recent development, is basically a software package which guides the CAI author through the programming process and virtually eliminates the need to know how to program the computer or to know a programming language of any kind.

The creation of CAI authoring systems is an attempt to automate the CAI authoring process. The progenitors of this approach seem to have recognized that many people who might otherwise be able to write CAI are prevented from doing so because they do not have the time to develop or maintain computer programming skill. These systems are but one example of the growing "friendliness" of microcomputers. It is, after all, in the interest of microcomputer manufacturers, software vendors and others to have microcomputers become easier for the layperson to use, and therefore that is exactly what is happening.

The CAI author is led through the authoring process one step at a time. Most systems are based on a simple "traditional" CAI model (if one can apply the word **traditional** to something as new as CAI). In the typical system, the CAI author is provided with options from which he or she can choose. The author is allowed to enter text to be displayed for the student to read, and can then choose to enter a question to be asked of the student. Having asked a question, the author is asked to enter any or all correct answers he will accept. Next, the author may be asked to enter anticipated wrong answers. The author may also be prompted by the system to decide how many times the student will be allowed to attempt each question, the hints that may be provided, or even how long the student may take to answer each question. The system will then take it from there and create the lesson segment, complete with directions to the student. All control functions will be executed by the system automatically.

Such systems are in their infancy; they have their shortcomings. For example, at the present state of the art, they lock the CAI author in to one model of CAI (even if it is the one most people would use anyway). They use up a lot of memory, are hard to revise, and do not keep very complete records of student performance or program performance. However, it should be said in their defense, they do what they set out to do. They permit a person with very little computer knowledge to write functional CAI very rapidly. We can look for giant improvements in these systems in the immediate future.

Another approach is to use a special purpose CAI author language. It does not do anything for the author automatically, but it does make programming CAI materials much more efficient than it would be with a more general purpose computer language. Typically, it only takes a few hours to become functional with such a language.

A CAI author language allows the CAI author much more flexibility than does a CAI authoring system. The author is much freer (although not completely free) to choose the CAI model he or she will use.

The third approach is to use a general purpose computer language. This approach requires a great deal more time to develop proficiency. However, the payoff is that you will have much more freedom to innovate, and your programs will be much more efficient both in speed and in the utilization of memory.

Which approach you will use to the issue of computer languages should be determined by a number of factors. For example, how soon do you want to be able to produce serviceable programs? How much time do you want to spend in developing your skills? How much time do you want to put into maintaining your skills? It is quite true of programming skill that "if you don't use it, you lose it."

If you plan to sell or receive a royalty from your programs, they will probably have to be written in at least a CAI authoring language. You may not have to do it all yourself, however. It is common to employ "coders," who simply transform your written text into whatever language is required.

It would be quite sensible to start with a CAI authoring system, move up to a CAI language, and then go on to a general computer programming language. In this way, you could keep up your motivation, and produce some useful products along the way.

Learn Which Characteristics of Microcomputers You Can Use for CAI

Generally speaking, the development of the capabilities of microcomputers has followed the direction of the development of large computers, albeit at a very tiny fraction of the cost. It is quite likely that this trend will continue.

Chapter 3 of this book is designed to save you a great deal of time and improve your efforts at writing CAI courseware as well by introducing you quickly to the range of microcomputer capabilities that represent the state of the art in microcomputer CAI. The intention is to help you avoid a problem that many new CAI authors have — that is, seizing on just a few of the many capabilities of the microcomputer and overusing them to the exclusion of others. The result is that their lessons are a little dull and monotonous. The ideal is to experiment and develop a repertoire of techniques

10

which fully exploit the strengths of state of the art microcomputers.

Develop a Knowledge of the Systems Approach

Much of the success of CAI lessons depends upon systematic design, development, and refinement methods. The collective, pragmatic wisdom of the systems approach provides an effective framework for this. You may already have sufficient familiarity with the systems approach as it relates to the creation of CAI. If not, you will find a brief, but appropriate, survey of the systems approach as it applies to CAI in Chapter 4.

Develop Your Instructional Writing Style

Instructional writing, particularly when it is done to create CAI lessons, is considerably different from most other forms of writing. The extent to which you understand this difference and use this understanding in your writing can affect the effectiveness of your lessons a great deal.

Chapter 5 is intended to help you make some of the necessary changes in your writing style and, perhaps more importantly, in your philosophy about writing.

Develop Your Repertoire of CAI Frame Styles

The most critical basic element of a CAI lesson is the frame. Frame is somewhat synonymous with question, but not quite. It can also be thought of as about the same as a step of the program, but not exactly.

There are many ways in which a frame can be designed. The richness and variety of frame styles which a CAI author has command of can make a great deal of difference in the quality, student acceptance, efficiency, and effectiveness of his lessons. Chapter 6 is intended to give you a head start in this area by providing an understanding of the basic design principles of good frame construction. The chapter will also provide some examples of good frames (technically called frame protocols). Some do's and don'ts are also provided to keep you out of trouble and save you time.

Develop Your CAI Design Skills

The effectiveness and revisability of your CAI lessons can be greatly enhanced if you learn some basic principles of CAI lesson design. The design of a lesson must be matched to the content of the lesson, the intended student population, and the ultimate purpose to which the students will put their new knowledge or skills.

Chapter 7 will introduce the basic principles of CAI lesson design, and it will also illustrate the main types of design which you will want to utilize.

Validate and Perfect Your Courseware

The only way to really know if your CAI lessons are effective is to test them on students. The process of testing and revising programs is technically called "validation." Validation techniques have been improved through years of development by instructional programmers and CAI authors. Chapter 8 will help you to take advantage of this experience as you validate your own CAI lessons.

The field of CAI is very diverse. There have been many years of development work on large computers in different locations and on different brands of computers. Some of these people shared their experiences and knowledge with each other, but many were unaware of the others or were otherwise not disposed to communicating their experiences with others.

Develop a Capacity to Create CAI Lessons

You will want to develop some systematic procedural steps to employ in the developmental process. Chapter 9 illustrates some proven techniques for the developmental process which you may wish to adopt.

Market Your Skills

Chapter 11 will help you to explore some of the ways you can derive compensation for your skills as a CAI author. There are many ways in which this can be done. The important thing is to be aware of all your alternatives in order to make an intelligent choice, or choices. It is also important to move quickly, since the CAI authorship field is a strong seller's market at this time and, although it is likely to remain so for a long time, there will no doubt come a time when it becomes quite competitive and experience and a track record of quality production will be important.

Market Your Courseware

Chapter 11 will help you to discover ways to sell or publish and draw royalties from your CAI courseware. There are many options in this area, since it is now a "seller's market." Early decisions are critical because they can affect your further activities in the field. Be careful not to damage your reputation by distributing your courseware too soon, before it is fully operational.

Be cautious also, about long-range commitments to a single publisher. Some CAI authors, in their zeal to take advantage of an offer of a "free" microcomputer, have signed agreements which seriously compromise their own property rights to all future software that they may write.

Plan to Acquire Your Own Microcomputer System

In order to have the freedom that you need to create CAI lessons, you would probably be well advised to invest in your own microcomputer system.

Plan to Participate in the Future of the Most Exciting Game in Town

The form of CAI will surely change as large numbers of people become involved in its production and utilization. The more solid your grounding in the fundamental principles and theory of CAI, the better equipped you are to play a major role in determining the future of CAI. Join me in a speculative look at the future of microcomputer CAI, as I envision it, in Chapter 12.

SOME ADDITIONAL THOUGHTS

There is something infectious about working with microcomputers. Almost everyone who works with them is won over. Even people who were reluctant, fearful, resentful, or even hostile at first, seem to quickly grow fond of their micro. Perhaps it is the micro's small size, and relative simplicity that gives people the feeling that it is more on a "human scale" than are the large computers. Perhaps it is the "friendliness"

13

manufacturers are able to build into them and software developers are able to enhance. At any rate, they are becoming extremely well accepted, and the interaction of microcomputers and users of all types is becoming a synergistic, almost symbiotic, relationship.

For purposes of comparison, it seems to me that only 10 percent of what makes a good CAI author has anything to do with computers or computer knowledge. The remainder has to do with a knowledge of how people learn, and with creativity. To me, creating CAI is more like writing poetry than it is like anything else. In both CAI and poetry, one has to appreciate the importance of using words in ways that achieve specific results. One must have the creativity to think up options and the endurance to persevere and keep writing and rewriting until the desired result is obtained. This book is designed to make it easier for you to achieve the "other 90 percent."

There is an interesting debate regarding whether there is more money to be made in manufacturing microcomputer hardware, distributing hardware, creating software, distributing software, creating CAI courseware, or distributing CAI coursware. When all things are considered, such as manufacturing costs, advertising, transportation, insurance, and so forth, I believe it makes sense for the CAI author to confine his or her activities to the development of CAI courseware and to let other specialized professionals in other organizations, such as publishers, carry out the other roles.

2

WHAT IS CAI?

Computer assisted instruction is an amazing term. Most people think they have a good idea of what it means. And yet, at this point in time, very few people (even teachers) have ever been a student in a CAI lesson, let alone written a CAI lesson or used one in their classroom. Nevertheless, I think it is fair to say that the tradition of CAI as it has evolved so far on large, mainframe computers has provided for most of us a model, if not a definition, of CAI.

To most of us CAI means a student sitting in front of the video-style screen of a computer terminal, or, equally likely now, a microcomputer. The computer largely controls the process, presenting material to the student for him or her to read and then periodically giving the student a question to answer or a problem to solve. The student then communicates his or her answer to the computer through a typewriterlike keyboard. In effect, the computer tutors or drills the student on the lesson material, keeping a record of the student's performance and producing a "grade," if desired.

There is some confusion in many people's minds about the relationship between CAI — computer assisted instruction — and CMI — computer managed instruction. The distinction is largely one of convention, because from a functional standpoint the two terms could be interchanged.

The convention is that CAI refers to a process in which the computer is actually the prime deliverer of the instruction, whereas CMI refers to a process in which the computer only "manages" the delivery of instruction.

In CMI, the computer is typically used to administer tests, grade them, and to assist in the development of an instructional prescription for the remediation of any knowledge deficiencies that are discovered. The computer is then used for retesting and even for record keeping and report writing. However, in a CMI application, the actual instruction is done by means other than those using computers. Most CAI includes at least a minimum amount of CMI, but, of course, not the other way around.

Within the broad rubric of CAI there are several subcategories, or types of CAI. The most common type is "tutorial" which is described above. However, another very common type is "drill-and-practice," which is much like electronic flashcards as used in learning the basic arithmetic skills, spelling, or other rote learning applications.

A definition of CAI which I prefer is the following: CAI is the direct use of the computer for the facilitation and certification of learning — that is, using the computer to make learning easier and more likely to occur (facilitation), as well as using the computer to create a record proving that learning has occurred (certification).

HISTORY OF CAI

The first computers were more marvelous than useful. They were expensive, not very reliable and no one really knew how to use them.

16

In the very early days of computers, it very likely did not occur to anyone, even those who developed the computer that such a thing as CAI would ever exist. The computer was originally seen as a very fast "number cruncher." The use of computers to manipulate alphabetic information came much later, and the idea of CAI came much later still.

The history of computer usage is to some extent a story of the search for economy within a very expensive technology. Most of the developments in the field can be seen as attempts to get more useful work performed by the computer.

Originally, computers were used to run one program at a time, with the computer operator stopping the computer to unload the previous run and to load the next program. Then, programs were put into batches to run continuously for longer periods of time. This produced an economy since the computer didn't have to be stopped as often. Another development in efficiency of computers was the dual job stream, which meant that the computer didn't have to be stopped at all, since one job stream was always running, even while the other one was being reloaded.

Another major development in the way computers are used was time sharing. In this process the computer is fitted with multiple terminals, all of which can share the computer. This is possible because the computer is so much faster than human operators that it can serve all of the terminals, and the degradation in service (response speed) is so slight that none of the users notices it. At least that's the theory. In practice there is a severe upper limit on the number of terminals that can be served by a single computer. The economy effected by time sharing comes from dividing the cost of the computer by the number of users. On paper, impressive economies can be achieved.

Nevertheless, it was time sharing and the promise of great economies that began to suggest the idea that CAI might some day be economical. However, one more, major element was needed to make CAI effective if not economical — that element was software, or programs to manage the computer and make it run the user's programs.

In the beginning computers were typically programmed by the engineers who created them. Since computers work on the binary numbering system, all programs were originally written in 0's and 1's. It was a very laborious process and was completely arbitrary. These languages are now referred to as "machine languages," although at the time they were not, since there were no other languages for them to be confused with.

The first major improvement in computer languages was the assembly language. The assembly language had the great advantage of being written, at least in part, in alphabetic letters, which meant that instructions could be made mnemonic. For example, a "move" instruction

17

might be written, "MV." The mnemonic assembly language was probably more responsible than any other factor for the initial development of the profession of programming. It meant that nonengineers could program the computers. Computer manufacturers were so impressed by the improvements represented by assembly languages that they gave them names like "EASYCODER" and "AUTOCODER."

Groups of users, rather than manufacturers were responsible for the first examples of the so-called higher level languages such as FORTRAN and COBOL. FORTRAN is an acronym for FORmula TRANslation. FORTRAN was designed for mathematical applications and reads much like algebraic formulas. COBOL is an acronym for COmmon Business Oriented Language and, of course, is specialized for use in business data processing.

The promise of CAI prompted some manufacturers to create a specialized language for CAI authors. Most of the CAI author languages are very similar. While some of the earliest CAI was written in assembly language, most authors probably switched to a CAI author language as soon as they were available. CAI author languages were much preferred, since they saved a great deal of time. One CAI author language instruction might take the place of twenty-five or more assembly language instructions. Furthermore, the CAI author language was more **mnemonic** with respect to the instructional process. That is, the specific code chosen bore a specific ralationship to the thing it stood for, such as some letters in common, making it more easily remembered. For example, RD might mean, "The following text is to be read only and requires no response." QU might mean "The following material is a question. Set up the conditions to judge a response." CA might mean, "The following item will be accepted as a correct response to the preceding question."

The CAI author language saved CAI authors time and allowed them to focus their activities on instructional logic and the writing of lessons rather than on computer programming. It also helped the authors, who in many cases were not too well acquainted with the pedagogical aspects of the lessons, to structure technically adequate lessons, albeit in a frankly behaviorist mode.

The fact that all early CAI author languages employ a behaviorist model is no doubt a result of the fact that most of the pioneers in the CAI field were originally programmed instruction practitioners. And, of course, programmed instruction was an application of behaviorist principles to learning needs.

Noting this relationship, some early critics of CAI contended that it amounted to little more than using the computer as an "electronic page turner." Some drill-and-practice CAI was described, even worse, as "electronic flash cards." These pejorative remarks carried all the more impact in view of the extreme cost of early computers.

18

Several large-computer manufacturers deserve credit for, in effect, subsidizing the development of CAI. IBM, for example, built about a dozen model 1500 computer systems which were intended exclusively for CAI. They were placed in university settings for the most part and were used to gain experience in CAI. They were, in effect, small (by today's standards), time-shared systems with fifteen or so terminals, dedicated to CAI use.

Control Data Corporation deserves much credit as well. They have subsidized and kept alive the largest CAI network ever developed. Called PLATO, it is perhaps the premier example of large-scale time-shared CAI systems and has served many purposes, not the least of which is the training of CAI authors. Many of the people who are now knowledgable about CAI received their training on the PLATO system.

PLATO also serves as a research vehicle. Control Data Corporation provides a large sum of money each year to be awarded as research grants to scholars investigating, or developing, various aspects of CAI on the PLATO system.

It is interesting to note that the latest version of the PLATO terminal is, in effect, a stand-alone microcomputer which has communications capability as well. By using the communications mode primarily to transmit the lesson material back and forth in high speed bursts, and then using the terminal in the stand-alone mode as students actually work through the lessons, a great deal of telephone time and central computer time is saved.

The advent of minicomputers allowed some companies to assemble rather inexpensive, small time-shared systems. These systems have proven to be cost effective enough to be applied in many areas. They are particularly useful and cost effective in very technical areas, in which traditional instructional methods are quite expensive.

ENTER MICROCOMPUTERS

The setting described in the preceding section existed at the time of the introduction of microcomputers. The microcomputer has so many advantages over all preexisting forms of computers that it is formidable competition indeed for its predecessors.

Microcomputers are marketed to the individual end user: a hobbyist, a teacher, a small-business person — people who will themselves be using the computer. Large computers were and are marketed to decision makers in large organizations who in most cases do not use the computer themselves. The actual computer use is left up to a cadre of "data processing people." The decision to purchase a computer is based on many factors, such as the minimum size needed for the largest job to be run, security, expandability, serviceability, and so on. It is seldom based upon ease of programming and operation. At the very least, if ease of use is considered, it is in the context of the considerable skills of the available data processing staff.

The marketing thrust of both the microcomputer manufacturers and the microcomputer software producers has resulted in microcomputers which are very simple to operate and software which demands as little expertise as possible on the part of the user. The term which has become popular to describe this trend is "friendliness." The effort to make the microcomputer friendlier is continuing with very good results.

MICROCOMPUTER CAI AUTHOR LANGUAGES

One of the payoffs of the friendliness effort is a simpler form of high-level CAI author language. COMMON PILOT is the name of one of the most popular. The producers of COMMON PILOT felt that the preexisting CAI author languages which were written for large computers, were, of course, written for professional CAI authors and were, as a result, undesirably complex. Professional authors could afford to take the time to learn a complex language and would spend the time necessary to maintain the skill.

They also felt that earlier languages locked authors into a behaviorist learning model which, while it reflected the biases of most earlier CAI authors, was now a little out of fashion, if not out of date. In my opinion, these efforts resulted in a CAI author language which is slightly simpler to use, but at the cost of some rather desirable mnemonics. I cannot see that they escaped the influence of the behaviorists, however, even if that were a worthy goal, and I'm not convinced it is.

The big advantage of the CAI author language, as I see it, is that it saves the CAI author time. It is about six times faster to create CAI lessons using a language like PILOT (and there are several others which are very similar) than it would be to use a more general purpose language like BASIC.

A second advantage is that it is still quite mnemonic and structures the CAI author's thinking, probably resulting in better lessons which are easier to update.

A third advantage is that programs written in a PILOT-type language are somewhat easier to run on computers other than those for which they were originally written. At least that is one of the goals. I am not sure how well it has been achieved yet.

In practice, I have found that the effectiveness of PILOT-like languages is limited. For some people, it is still too complex. They do not have the time (or the talent, perhaps) to develop and maintain adequate facility with PILOT. Other people find it too simple and too restrictive, preferring instead to use BASIC or even an assembly language. An assembly language runs faster and uses less memory than either BASIC or PILOT.

COMPUTER-ASSISTED-INSTRUCTION AUTHORING SYSTEMS

I find it useful to distinguish between CAI authoring **languages** such as PILOT, and CAI authoring **systems** such as I will discuss now. PILOT is a high-level language, a specialized language, but still a language. CDS 1, produced by Bell and Howell, is a **system**. CDS 1 does much more for the CAI author than PILOT does.

CAI authoring systems, of which CDS 1 is but one example, represent a further step in the effort to make computers friendlier. These CAI authoring systems are, in part, examples of a new class of software, the "menu-driven" software system.

In a menu-driven system, the objective seems to be to eliminate the need for the user to have any computer programming skills whatsoever. In such a system, the user is presented with options on the screen from which he or she simply selects the one that best fits his or her needs. By presenting the user with a series of simple questions to answer, the computer controls the process of gaining the information it needs to automatically create a program which will accomplish the user's objectives.

The first generation of CAI authoring systems were limited in capability, used unconscionable amounts of memory, were prone to bugs which rendered them inoperable until "regenerated" back at the national headquarters of the vendor and, most unforgivable of all, they sometimes "lost" the data, or lessons that users had worked so hard to produce. In addition to the inherent problems in implementing such a technology, the avarice of the vendors prompted them to build the software in such a way that it could not be copied, even to backup lessons.

Despite all the problems the first examples of CAI authoring systems had, they also had strengths. Just as a CAI authoring language such as PILOT enables the CAI author to create CAI lessons up to six times faster than would be the case with a more general language such as BASIC, the CAI authoring systems are more efficient for the CAI author than CAI authoring languages.

Fortunately we are already into a second generation of CAI authoring systems for microcomputers. Many of the earlier bugs have been worked out, and some methods have been found for licensing the software, thus satisfying

21

the vendor's needs for a profit and protection of copyright, but not interfering with fair use of the systems.

THE THEORETICAL UNDERPINNINGS OF CAI

So far we have looked at the mechanics, (or electronics, as it were) of CAI. Now we will examine the theoretical aspects of the instructional design considerations. CAI owes its greatest debt to behavioral psychology, since it was the predominant school of thought in psychology at the time CAI originated.

The CAI model which predominates today is based on the **law of effect**, which is also the basis of behavioral psychology. Because the early behaviorist Thorndike is credited with its discovery, it is often called **Thorndike's law of effect.** The main assumption of the law is simple: Behavior which is followed by pleasure is more likely to be repeated than behavior which is not so followed.

The law of effect has been used most widely in animal training. The trainer gives the animal a cue — the **stimulus** or **S.** The animal performs the desired behavior — the **response** or **R.** The trainer gives the animal a reward — the **reinforcement.**" By reinforcing the animal for making the correct response (or successively closer approximations of it), the probability of the correct response occurring again in the presence of the stimulus is increased. This process — stimulus, response, and reinforcement — is often referred to simply as **S-R theory.**

S-R theory has been widely tested in animal studies. It proves the law of effect to be valid beyond any reasonable doubt — for animals. However, psychologists did not undertake years of elaborate animal studies because they were curious about animal learning. This work was done because it is assumed that animal learning is much like human learning. The advantage of using animal subjects is that it is cheaper, faster, easier, and raises fewer ethical problems to work with animals than to work with humans. The disadvantage is that animal learning and human learning are not identical processes.

Many people, including many psychologists, have serious doubts about the validity of applying the law of effect or S-R methods to human learning. Most agree that the law applies to simple knee-jerk types of behavior. The doubt occurs in regard to higher-order cognitive and verbal learning such as we are usually concerned with in CAI.

Nevertheless B. F. Skinner, a professor at Harvard University, became famous, in part, for applying S-R theory to human learning. It took a form called

programmed learning, programmed instruction, or **PI.** In PI, the student is given a question — the **stimulus.** He or she answers — the **response.** Then feedback is provided (in a good program the student will nearly always be correct). The theory is that the student will be rewarded and learning will be reinforced by the mere feedback that the answer is correct.

The reason for doubt is that there is no solid evidence that the law of effect works for higher-order cognitive human learning. It is even hard to see how an experiment could be set up to test this. If a PI student gave a correct answer and got feedback that it was correct, it would be hard to attribute future performance, good or bad, solely to the fact that he or she got positive feedback earlier.

Still another fact confuses the issue. There is some evidence that students are **less** likely to get the same question wrong again than they are to miss one he previously answered correctly, particularly if a lot of attention is drawn to the error (and there usually is).

However, all of this would be an irrelevant academic argument if it were not for one fact. Most CAI authoring systems are based on the S-R model. They seem to assume that the law of effect is in full force in CAI. The options built into many CAI authoring systems make it easier to use S-R theory than not to. In fact, in a few systems the author is forced to use S-R theory.

Some of the newest CAI authoring systems were actually written in a deliberate attempt to free the author from such constraints. PILOT is one such example. However, even PILOT does not succeed entirely. Many authors feel so strongly about the issue that they will use no CAI authoring system, preferring instead to use some more general method, writing all their CAI in standard programming languages such as BASIC or PASCAL.

There are many refinements of PI and CAI which derive their validity from the theoretical work of behavioral scientists as well. For example, the main characteristics of programmed instruction are the following:

1. Small steps

2. Active responding

3. Immediate feedback

A great many doctoral dissertations and research grants have been earned investigating aspects of behavioral theory as they relate to PI and CAI. This activity has yielded a great deal of positive direction for CAI which carefully relates research and practice.

However, much of the advice and many of the caveats offered to PI and CAI authors are based on little more than analogy and common sense.

As much as behavioral psychology has contributed to CAI (and no doubt will continue to contribute for some time to come), there are newer schools of thought in psychology which are in a position to contribute much as well. The most promising are the ideas which view the human brain and thought processes as analogous to the computer itself.

There has been a resurgence of interest in the cognitive school of psychology. One of the new developments in this field has a great deal of promise for CAI. It is called **cognitive monitoring**. It holds that what we humans really do when we learn is to develop better and better means of analyzing and controlling our own thought processes, within our own heads.

Referring to the process as **cognitive monitoring**, these psychologists are interested in the strategies which their subjects develop for accomplishing such things as learning or remembering. They are also interested in how we learn to use feedback on our performance to improve future performance under similar but not necessarily identical conditions.

I think that cognitive psychology in general, and cognitive monitoring in particular, will have much to offer the CAI author in years to come.

LIKELY FUTURE DIRECTIONS OF CAI

Large-computer CAI has served as a model for most of the CAI which has been written for microcomputers thus far. However, to a rather great extent, the modeling has been only imitative, copying the form of large-computer CAI rather than working with the underlying principles. I expect this to change, and I expect to see considerable research into the effectiveness of CAI and the development of more effective models. I also expect to see the development of a considerable and respectable body of knowledge regarding CAI.

While much of what is going on today in microcomputer CAI is based closely on what has gone before (on large computers), there is also a great deal of innovation occurring. This is certain to result in continued, and indeed accelerated, development of new models of CAI. I'm certain that models will be developed which are far superior to those which are in existence today — models which will more fully exploit the unique strengths of the computer and will reduce the rather great amount of human effort required to produce CAI courseware using the courseware development methods which predominate today.

In spite of the new models of CAI that are certain to be developed, the traditional model of CAI is likely to be with us for quite sometime, indeed, for some applications it may always be appropriate. There are many ways in which the microcomputer can be used to make the CAI authoring process easier, using more computer assistance for the authoring process, even within the traditional model.

A large part of the reason that there is such a shortage of CAI courseware at this time is that it is so costly in time and money to produce CAI courseware for the CAI models which prevail today. Estimates vary as to the cost, but a ratio of **two hundred hours** to produce, field-test and validate a **one-hour** lesson segment is not uncommon.

There is clearly a need to reduce the time needed to produce CAI courseware. One obvious solution is to enlist the computer to help the author. We have seen earlier in this chapter how software, in the form of a CAI authoring system, can be used to speed up the coding process by as much as twelve times. Of course coding is only one part of the CAI lesson production process. The total CAI lesson creation process includes several other time-consuming processes as well.

Probably the most time-consuming process is the writing process. Fortunately, there are ways in which the microcomputer can help in this area as well. There are word processors which can be used to simplify the writing process mechanically. In addition, there are on-line dictionaries which can check spelling automatically. (Some of the programs we have seen sold commercially could definitely have benefited from an on-line dictionary.) There is software for large computers which will no doubt be scaled down for microcomputers, and which can automatically determine the readablility level of writing according to any one of a variety of standard indexes of readability or a combination thereof.

Related to readability level is the grade level of the material. The computer can one day be set up to help the CAI author to adjust a CAI lesson to the appropriate grade level quite easily.

Similarly, we will no doubt soon have thesauri which help us to find "just the right word" to use. One could even conceive of a directory which would help us select metaphors, analogies, and other forms of figurative language to enhance our CAI lessons.

Given the activity in the microcomputer market, I think we can expect the trend toward friendliness to continue. There will be many developments designed to assist the general user. There will also be specialized offerings to help the user engaged in specific computer applications. The CAI author will certainly be one of the specialists most catered to, since there is such a demand for CAI courseware.

3

MICROCOMPUTERS AND CAI

INTRODUCTION

Microcomputers have astonishing potential for use in CAI. The basic capability of microcomputers is being extended with each new generation of microcomputer manufactured. The power of microcomputers is also being extended by various hardware items manufactured to add to microcomputers. Another major element contributing to the rapid development of microcomputer capability is software. Improved operating systems, languages, and CAI authoring systems are being developed continuously.

In this chapter, the array of state-of-the-art capabilities of the kind of microcomputers most likely to be encountered in schools will be described. We will first step through the major CAI capabilities of the microcomputer in the simple logical order most frequently used in CAI lessons. Then, some of the more exotic capabilities of the microcomputer which can be exploited for CAI will be discussed. Finally, some of the less glamorous and less obvious features of the microcomputer will be treated.

In addition to discussing the capabilities of the microcomputer, we will also discuss the responsibilities of the CAI author and some of the elements of good technique which should be employed in writing CAI.

It is hoped that this chapter will help you to exploit the capabilities of the microcomputer and related software to create effective CAI.

The typical microcomputer on which this book is based is a stand-alone, 8-bit-byte microcomputer with up to 64k bytes of dynamic internal memory. It has a typewriter-like keyboard and a visual display either in the form of a television set or a specialized monitor. As an optional storage device, it may have either a cassette tape recorder or one or two mini-floppy disc drives. It is also assumed that various "off-the-shelf" accessories and hardware modification cards may be added to the microcomputer to enhance its capability beyond that provided by the manufacturer.

These basic capabilities of the microcomputer are the building blocks from which all CAI lessons are built.

DIRECTIONS

One of the most critical aspects of any CAI is the provision of clear and consistent directions to the student. It is important that the student know at all times what he or she is to do next. If directions are unclear, the student can waste a lot of time and lose respect for the program, not to mention losing patience and motivation. Remember, you will not always be there to "straighten things out." Your programs are like paintings. They must stand or fall on their own.

I was recently shown some some CAI which had been written by a person with good computer knowledge, but no background in CAI or educational technology. I was immediately struck by the complete absence of any directions to the student. When I commented about it, he said, "The instructor will tell them what they are expected to do." The lack of directions severely limits the usefulness of this program. The program cannot stand alone, but must always be used in a traditional classroom environment with a teacher present. Moreover, it puts an unnecessary burden on the teacher. In use, this program is likely to produce many delays for students — delays which can be destructive of motivation.

I have also seen many programs which provide no backup system if the student either fails to understand the directions or simply forgets them. It should not be possible for your students to "get lost" in your programs. It is your responsibility to do everything you can to insure that students always have a way out, and that it is known to them.

The need for extensive directions is decreased if procedures are kept consistent. If the student is to press the key marked RETURN to receive new information to read or to go on, make sure it is **always** the RETURN key that produces this result. Also, make sure that that **is** what it is marked on every machine your program may be run on. What is called the RETURN key on one machine may be marked ENTER, TRANSMIT, or perhaps SEND on other machines. One clever way around this problem is to direct the student to depress **any** key whatsoever to go on. Then, be sure you set the microcomputer up to accept the depression of any key as a signal to go on. Another common technique is to use the space bar since all keyboards have them and they are unlabeled.

In some of the newer CAI authoring systems, minimal directions are provided automatically. However, you may want to supplement these to make your lessons flow more smoothly for your students.

SUCCESSION

Many authors are tempted to put successive messages on the screen and have the succession occur automatically, using some sort of timing technique, such as an internal counter, to time the delay. If you use this technique, use it only in the beginning to control the succession of the first few messages. Then switch to student-controlled succession as soon as possible. There are three problems with the technique of automatic succession. The first is that it is almost impossible to time the delay so that it is correct for all or even a majority of students. The second is that the student is deprived of a sense of control. Finally, the computer may be made to look stupid, by accentuating the fact that CAI is all a preprogrammed, artificial process.

One technique that can be quite effective and should not be overlooked is to build up a screen display in successive stages.

For some materials, such as lists or something in which a sense of location is important, it may be sensible to have the screen "scroll" — that is, material that moves, usually from the bottom of the screen to the top. New material occurs at the bottom and then moves up to make room for succeeding material. When the old material gets to the top of the screen, it disappears. It is almost as if the screen were a window in front of a large sheet of material moving steadily upward behind it.

In some systems the provision is made for the student to have the ability to override the automatic control of screen succession and to go either forward or backward within the lesson. This is a desirable feature in most instructional settings, and it should become even more common in the future.

FORMAT

The display of even the smallest microcomputer can become crowded and therefore difficult to read when it is full or even close to being full. Therefore, it is generally considered better technique to put only a small amount on each screen at any one time. If you have a lot of material to be presented, it is better to break it up into short messages which can be presented successively. Writing for CAI causes most people to learn to write more succinctly. Some CAI authoring systems automatically limit the amount you can display on any one screen.

Feel free to use any portion of the screen. It is often better to put each new message in a different location on the screen than the previous message occupied, even though you have taken the previous message away. The reason for this is that some computers are so fast, that if the student looks away even briefly he or she may not realize that the message has changed. The eighty-column screen, in particular, is often felt to be too wide. You may therefore wish to use a narrower column width, centered on the screen, and perhaps consisting of several lines. In an ideal system, you might have the capacity to adjust display format to the student's reading style.

On most microcomputers, it is possible to select a larger character size. Of course, when you do, the line length and number of lines that can be displayed decreases accordingly. When preparing material for young children, this can be particularly appropriate.

QUESTIONS

Questions are a key element in most CAI as we know it. Therefore, the techniques for asking questions, judging student responses and responding to student responses are critical. Well-constructed questions have several characteristics which contribute to the success

29

of the CAI program. Good questions permit students to interact with the material in a way that provides practice, which leads to mastery. Good questions enable students to demonstrate to themselves and to others that they have mastered the material. Finally, good questions provide students a favorable "pain-to-gain ratio" — that is, their sense of progress is great enough to justify the effort they must put forth.

Anticipated Correct Answers

The CAI lesson must be prepared to judge student responses, usually by comparing them to anticipated correct answers supplied by the CAI author. At the simplest level, responses can be compared on a one-to-one basis with the exact and complete answer as provided by the CAI author.

However, often the student will supply an answer that is slightly different in form from that anticipated by the author even though it is still correct. The student might, for example, abbreviate the answer, spell it incorrectly, or otherwise construct the answer so that it will not exactly match the one the computer has been given by the author. Therefore, the CAI author should provide for more tolerance and flexibility in accepting an answer. For example, knowing that the correct first and last letters of the answer have been given is often enough evidence to conclude with a high degree of certainty that the answer is correct. Therefore, the CAI author may wish to make the answer contingent only on the first and last letters. This approach can minimize the effect of some misspelling and some abbreviation.

In other cases, there may be several distinct alternative answers, all of which are acceptable. The CAI author need only list them for the computer.

Another refinement which the CAI author can work with is to branch to different parts of the program for different answers. For example, the answer may be unquestionably correct, in which case the CAI author may branch the student to the most direct route through the program. Another answer may be nearly correct but betray a little confusion on the part of the student. The CAI author may branch this student to a remedial segment before going on.

In providing feedback, the CAI author has several options as well. The student may simply be told that the response is correct. He or she may be given a compliment. A nice touch is to have the computer play a simple little tune. Another approach is to provide some pleasant graphics or perhaps a brief animated show. Be careful, though, that your response acknowledgment techniques don't use up too much of the student's time.

Anticipated Wrong Answers

It is probably the handling of wrong answers that taxes CAI authors' capabilities the most. CAI authors must plan, in advance, almost in a vacuum, for whatever incorrect responses the student might make. They must also plan for as many incorrect answers as the student might give. They can never leave the student stranded.

By analyzing the question carefully, CAI authors can often anticipate a number of possible incorrect answers the student might give. Each of the incorrect answers might represent a different kind of misunderstanding. CAI authors may want to create a different remedial sequence to which the student may be branched for each type of wrong answer.

One common method of dealing with an incorrect response is to provide the student with a hint, and cycle him or her back to attempt the same question again. Oftentimes even the hint is omitted, and the student is simply cycled back, again and again. It sometimes seems as though the author felt that the student must answer each specific question exactly right before going on.

If the strategy of simple recycling does not work, the CAI author is often at a loss and chooses to "cop-out" by directing the student to "call the instructor." Don't do this. There is nothing sacred about any one specific question. Create alternative questions which are equivalent in function but which are worded differently or use a different format.

One technique for handling anticipated wrong answers is to condition the computer not to accept them. That is, even if the student types them, they will not stay on the screen. The concept behind this is that the student should not see incorrect material in print, or in lights, since it might be unintentionally reinforced.

A technique which has recently become quite popular is **answer marking**. If an answer is substantially correct, but is misspelled for example, the computer can simply "mark" the spelling error and then either accept or reject the answer. This method takes advantage of the opportunity to teach some subtle things and to shape the student's behavior.

Unanticipated Responses

No matter how much you know about the subject matter, no matter how good a programmer you are, no matter how well you study and anticipate alternatives, some students will still supply answers that you have not anticipated. The program will have no way of knowing if such answers are right or wrong.

There are various ways to handle this. You can say,

answer," or, "I don't recognize your answer" and then branch the student to another attempt at another question. You may also simply ask the student to rephrase the answer.

At any rate, play it safe and don't supply a message that will not fit the circumstance. It will only make the process look stupid and shake the student's confidence.

Null Response

There will be times when a student is simply unable to make any intelligent response. The directions to the student should cover this event, and the student should know at all times how to proceed, even if he or she can't answer the question. Normally it would be to type "help," or perhaps simply to press the ENTER key or whatever is the equivalent on the machine he or she is using. At any rate, you must provide for this "loose end." Surprisingly, some commercially distributed courseware does not.

Response Latency

One of the things that a computer is very good at is keeping track of time. Therefore, one very useful technique is to keep track of the time that a student spends deliberating about an answer. The time that elapses from the student's first opportunity to respond until he or she actually does respond is technically called **response latency.** There is considerable evidence to indicate that the longer it takes a student to make a response, the more likely the answer is to be wrong. Therefore, it can be a kindness to the student to measure the latency, and to provide hints or cues, or perhaps just ask the student if he or she would like help.

It would be a good idea to record the response latencies, particularly during the validation cycle, in order to use the information as a very **fine-grained** form of data upon which to base revision.

BRANCHING

We have mentioned **branching** several times. It simply means that the logical flow of the lesson will follow one or another of several alternative paths, depending upon which of several conditions is met. Sometimes, it simply means branching ahead, or skipping some parts of the lesson. Sometimes, it means doubling back to repeat some portion of the lesson.

Branching is a very important feature of CAI. Branching is a technique which makes good use of the computer's capability. While a lot of good lessons can be written without using branching, it is still a good technique with which to become competent. In Chapter 7 and Chapter 9 branching will be dealt with at length. Here, it is sufficient to realize that branching may either be done automatically as a contingency of student performance, or it may be openly provided as an opportunity for the student to make decisions affecting the course of his or her own study.

SPECIAL TECHNIQUES

On many microcomputers it is possible to create a condition called **inverse video**. That is, the area immediately around each character is lighted, and the character itself is unlit — black on white, rather than white on black, if you will. This technique is particularly helpful in creating a distinction between two kinds of information that appear on the screen. For example, the directions to the student might appear in inverse video at the top or bottom of the screen, and the lesson content might occur in regular video in the center section of the screen.

Another technique of highlighting is called **foreground/background**. What it amounts to is two levels of brightness for characters in the same display. It allows one or more words to be more brightly lit than the others. You might use it in place of underlining, since underlining is not typically available on microcomputers as yet.

On many microcomputers it is possible to make selected characters flash on and off, or **blink**. This technique can be used to highlight things. You might, for example, use it as a hint, causing a key word to flash either after a long delay or after the student has given an incorrect answer.

Graphics

The use of graphics in CAI is becoming more popular. Newer CAI authoring systems are making it easier to use graphics, but it is still quite awkward. It is wise to experiment with graphics nevertheless.

It is possible to produce a sense of motion in graphics by using multiple images and exploiting the automatic timing characteristics of the computer. One clever application of this is to provide a small cartoon character which shakes its head from side to side for an incorrect answer and up and down for a correct answer. A great deal can be done in this regard by an imaginative CAI author.

Speech Generation

There are two methods of generating speech directly on the microcomputer. Typically, both require that the microcomputer be modified by the addition of pieces of hardware. The first method requires that the CAI author write very painstaking computer code for the synthetic production of speech. The result is usually very artificial sounding.

The second method involves what amounts to a digital recording of speech. This is by far the more natural sounding and the more convenient of the two methods.

Both methods use incredible amounts of memory at the current state of the art. I think we will see major advances in this technology in the near future. However, for certain applications, such as teaching spelling or for second languages, these methods can be quite justifiable.

Speech Recognition

The ability of microcomputers to recognize human speech is quite effective. However, it is limited in at least two ways. First, it is limited to thirty to sixty words. Second, the computer must be "trained" to recognize one specific speaker at a time. This can be awkward and time consuming. However, there is no doubt that it is efficient from the student's point of view. It should be pointed out that at the present state of the art, the computer can be very slow to analyze what is "heard." This technology will certainly be improved in the future and promises to be extremely useful to the CAI author.

Light Pens

There is one attachment which can be added to microcomputers which greatly extends the usefulness of the microcomputer for CAI purposes. It is the light pen. The light pen usually requires that an electronic "card" be installed in the microcomputer. A wire connects the light pen and the card. When the light pen has been installed and the microcomputer has been properly programmed, it is possible to detect where the light pen is touched to the screen. In an operational sense in CAI, it means that a student can select an answer on the screen by merely pointing the light pen at it rather than by depressing one or more keys. One advantage is response economy — it is quicker and easier to point than to enter a response through the keyboard. This feature is especially useful with small children or with students who have limited finger dexterity.

Auxiliary Equipment Control

The microcomputer can readily be used to control auxiliary equipment, such as tape recorders, videotape recorders, videodisc recorders (or players), as well as motion picture and slide projectors. Some of the new CAI authoring systems are particularly useful for this.

To be controlled by a microcomputer, the video recorder, audio recorder, or whatever device is used must be specially made for remote control. Most major brands of equipment make one or more models of each device specially equipped for this purpose. You will also need to add an electronic circuit card to your microcomputer which is specially designed. The card will most likely come with some software to be used with it and some instructions telling how to program for it.

RECORD KEEPING

There are three basic reasons for record keeping in CAI. One is to have a record of student performance for purposes of grading the student or determining his or her future educational options. It is of great utility to teachers if the courseware keeps a permanent record of student accomplishment. In this way, the teacher does not have to copy the student's performance statistics from the screen and record it somewhere else each time the student signs off the microcomputer. I am certain that if teachers were asked to choose between two pieces of CAI courseware which were equal except for the fact that one kept good records and the other didn't, the one which kept good records would be chosen every time.

The second use of record keeping is to control branching and the course of the student through the CAI lesson. If a record of student performance is kept, the student can be branched to alternative parts of the program based on an analysis of performance.

The third reason is the one that is the most important to the CAI author — that is, record keeping provides a basis for the revision of CAI lessons. For this purpose, it is important to have detailed information regarding which items were missed, as well as the specific correct and incorrect answers which were given.

Record keeping is an important capability of the computer which is usually not exploited fully. Most CAI authoring systems only keep track of a cumulative score of right and wrong answers. Typically, there is not even any provision for keeping track of which answers were missed, let alone keeping track of what the wrong answers were. The reason for this is in part the limited memory space available on most microcomputers.

It is unfortunate that this information is not kept, since it is invaluable in the important process of revising CAI lessons which is referred to by the technical term **validation.** Validation is treated in detail in chapter 8.

4

SYSTEMS THINKING AND CAI

A CAI lesson is a very complex thing to produce. Several highly sophisticated technologies must be integrated in such a way as to produce an organically complete entity which is capable of achieving a specific result. The CAI author must draw upon several fields of knowledge to put together an effective lesson. The CAI author faces quite a challenge. He or she must become knowledgeable enough of all of these technologies to be able to create a CAI lesson which is an effective teaching instrument. To do so, the CAI author must keep track of many different entities and optimize the development of the lesson. All of the parts of the lesson must be kept in proportion — none may predominate at the expense of the others.

One of the best strategies yet devised for accomplishing this is the **systems approach.** The systems approach has undergone parallel development in many different fields over the last thirty years or so. Several of these fields claim authorship, but its true origins are hard to trace.

The adoption of a systems approach will help to ensure that the CAI lessons which are developed are well structured. Good structure makes lessons easier to revise and improve. In fact, a poorly structured CAI lesson whose design is obscure or lacking in the beginning can become hopelessly confusing during the revision process.

We will examine briefly the various areas of human knowledge with which the CAI author must either become familiar or seek assistance in order to produce effective CAI lessons.

1.   The subject matter that will make up the lesson.

The CAI author must either have a good knowledge of the content of the lesson or seek out the assistance of someone who has. It is not uncommon for the CAI author to rely on a subject matter specialist (SMS). Individuals who author CAI for a living cannot possibly be knowledgeable in all of the fields in which they are required to author lessons. Such persons have developed their techniques for working with an SMS to a very high level.

2.   Learning theory.

The parent science of CAI is psychology, particularly behaviorism and its associated learning theory. A considerable body of knowledge has accumulated over the years that can be of great assistance to the CAI author. The CAI author should either be acquainted with this field or seek the assistance of someone who is. The individual who lacks such knowledge can of course acquire such knowledge or rely on his or her own intuition. However, the results are almost certain to be better if expert knowledge is available. One of the purposes of this book is to provide a limited amount of the knowledge available from learning theory.

3. Instructional systems design technology.

Many people feel that instructional systems design (ISD) constitutes a profession in itself. Some universities have degree programs in ISD.

4. Computer science.

Computer knowledge is rapidly becoming easier to acquire. In the beginning, computers were a product of universities. As corporations began to commercialize computers, it soon became too costly for all but a few very elite universities to participate. The best training in computers was available only through corporations. Now the situation has come full circle, and universities are providing excellent training and producing some excellent people. Reasonably good training is available from a variety of other sources as well, and as a result, there are many good people around. Therefore, it is increasingly less important for CAI authors to have a great deal of computer knowledge themselves — they can now readily seek assistance from computer specialists.

It is evident, just from the short list of knowledge prerequisites for the authorship of CAI lessons listed here, that it would be very hard for any one person to have all the knowledge necessary. Perhaps, in years to come, academic programs will be available which develop all these skills. However, for now, one of the best approaches is to work in teams.

I strongly advise the CAI author to become acquainted with the concepts and procedures of the systems approach and apply them conscientiously in the creation of CAI lessons. The systems approach is probably the best strategy yet devised for ensuring that a complex system (such as a CAI lesson) can be made to work.

GENERAL SYSTEMS MODELS

There are lots of books on systems, however, most of them try to apply to so many areas that they wind up applying to none.

The general model of the systems approach involves five parts.

1. Analyze problem.
2. Specify required outcome.
3. Design system.
4. Create system.
5. Test and revise system.

While the preceding list appears to be quite simple, it turns out in practice to be quite difficult to apply directly in any particular area. It is necessary to examine the specifics of the application of the systems approach in the instructional systems design area in detail in order to apply it successfully. This chapter is intended to help you with that process.

THE SYSTEMS APPROACH AS IT APPLIES TO CAI

What I will attempt to do is apply the central ideas of systems thinking to the specific task of writing CAI lessons for microcomputers.

The systems approach, as it applies to the development of CAI lessons, involves the following entities:

1. Front-end analysis
2. Outcome representation
3. Lesson design
4. Lesson creation
5. Lesson validation

FRONT-END ANALYSIS

Front-end analysis (FEA) probably arose as a result of the all too common experience of developing an instructional strategy which might include very expensive materials development only to find that the chosen approach was inappropriate and ineffective. Enough individuals and organizations have been "burned" by this problem that a virtual science (if not a religion) of front-end analysis has developed. The Department of Defense, for example, requires that all training projects include a very complete front-end analysis carried out as specified in a very large book on FEA which they have produced.

Determination of the Appropriateness of Instructional Approach

In a typical FEA application, a training specialist is given a problem in human performance to solve. After having decided whether or not the performance problem is a knowledge deficiency, and, whether or not that deficiency can likely be resolved by an instructional approach, the training specialist must decide which is the best instructional medium to use. CAI would be the right approach only in a certain percentage of cases.

However, in this book I am making an assumption that the reader's situation will be the reverse. That is, the reader will have decided that he or she wishes to write a CAI lesson, and then will be faced with the problem of selecting appropriate subject matter. Therefore, I will discuss from this perspective some of the considerations one should make in selecting subject matter. This is a crucial matter since not all subject matter lends itself to CAI format, at least not at this state of the CAI art.

Specification of the Beginning Conditions

In order to write CAI, the author must know some of the relevant characteristics of the students who will use the program and the conditions under which it will be used. At a minumum he or she will need to know the grade level of the students and whether or not the program will be used in a classroom, along with other materials.

The Lesson Rationale

In developing a CAI lesson, I prefer to start with a written rationale. The act of writing the rationale causes one to think the problem through more clearly. The rationale communicates more succinctly, efficiently, and holistically than any other method of development.

Typically, the CAI author knows much of what should go into a rationale long before he or she knows many of the other features the lesson is likely to have. For example, you will probably know the target population, the microcomputer to be used, the subject matter, the grade level, the approximate length, the time and other resources available, the authoring approach that will be used, and so forth. This kind of information communicates a lot about your proposed lesson.

The existence of a good rationale makes it much easier to accomplish the other steps in describing the lesson which must follow. In addition, the rationale will improve the way in which the other components communicate.

OUTCOME SPECIFICATION

In instructional planning, communicating about instruction and in instructional systems development, it is typically necessary to represent subject matter in some shorthand manner for convenience. If, for example, you wish to obtain a contract from a publisher before you go to the work of creating the entire CAI lesson, you will need to represent the lesson to the publisher in some way that communicates what the lesson will be like.

It is becoming more common to write CAI lessons in teams, since a team can be made up of members who will complement each other's skills. Good documentation of the proposed lesson facilitates the planning and the cooperative effort of the team. One could cite many additional circumstances which make it desirable to represent the lesson in some abbreviated symbolic way.

A variety of methods are often used to represent the lesson depending on the purpose. Rationales, task lists, objectives, topic lists, and other approaches are used, depending on the need.

Topic Lists

Topic lists are usually a good next step after writing the rationale. They are easy to write, easy to sort and manipulate, and topics form good units of association for subsequent planning. Topic lists facilitate and refine the process of determining what will and what won't be in the lesson. Determining the sequence of the lesson is also facilitated by a topic list.

Task Lists

For some kinds of lesson content, such as vocational areas in which the students will be expected to perform in certain specific ways after completing the lesson, task lists are preferable to topic lists.

There is a confusion that sometimes arises about the use of the term **task**. The confusion derives from the fact that the term is sometimes used to refer to **learning** tasks and at other times is used to refer to **job** tasks. Here, we are referring to learning tasks.

Task Analysis

The main value of using the learning tasks approach is that a well-developed technique called **task analysis** exists for examining the tasks in terms of the characteristics of the learning involved. Task analysis permits one to relate the task of learning a specific thing to a body of knowledge having to do with levels and categories of learning. Once the learning task has been well defined in these terms, it is relatively easy to choose an appropriate lesson format.

The technique of task analysis has been highly evolved in the ISD (instructional systems design) field. Through such techniques, a great deal of information about the content of the proposed lesson can be collected, represented, shared, and used in the development of the lesson. Some of it may also wind up in the permanent documentation which will accompany the finished lesson.

In a typical task analysis, each of the learning tasks is evaluated according to a set of criteria such as the following:

1. Importance
2. Learning level
3. Prerequisite skills required
4. Learning difficulty
5. Retention difficulty

This author has performed task analyses in which as many as 230 learning tasks were compared against as many as 40 criteria, resulting in 9200 separate pieces of information about the proposed learning material. That's quite a bit to know about the lesson material before even the first lesson component is written.

Criterion Frames

Criterion frames are essentially questions which are designed to test the progress of a student's understanding and readiness to move on within the lesson. They will be covered in detail in a later chapter, but it is sufficient to note here that they can be seen as serving the secondary purpose of documenting the intended content of the lesson.

Objectives

Objectives are a very useful form of representing the proposed content of a lesson. Thanks to the heavy emphasis that has been placed on the use of behavioral objectives over the last decade or two, nearly everyone has some skill in writing them.

There are some techniques for writing objectives which make the job of writing them somewhat easier while at the same time making the objectives more useful. I have found, for example, that if the objectives are conceived as having several parts, it is somewhat easier to assemble the parts. A complete and useful objective has the following components:

1. A topic (to which the objective refers)

2. The conditions (under which the objective is performed including such things as prerequisite skills)
3. An action statement (which must include a verb which describes an observable act on the part of the student)
4. Criteria (which must be met to satisfy the accomplishment of the objective).

I have found the form that follows (fig. 4-1) to be useful in developing objectives.

By constructing the objective from these components, the task is actually made easier, because you can fill in the pieces as you are able to acquire them. They are usually not all available from the same source, but rather from a variety of subject matter specialists and written sources.

Who Did What to Whom?

There is a confusion which frequently interferes with the process of writing objectives. It has to do with the subject as well as the object of the verb in the written objective itself. While the student is the subject and the subject matter or some other inanimate object is usually the object, many people get it mixed up and make the teacher or the instructional system the subject and the student the object. For example, one often sees objectives written which say something like the following: "I will get **them** to read chapter five."

The problem with such an objective is that it says nothing about what the student will retain from the lesson and gives us no guidance for either designing a lesson or evaluating a lesson. Such an objective is called a process objective, because it refers to and has meaning only in the context of the process of learning, and does not speak to the outcome of the learning. I find that the table that follows (table 4-1) helps me and some of the people I consult with to keep this straight.

You will notice from the table that it is possible to have the following four kinds of objectives within this scheme:

1. System (or teacher) process objectives (CELL A)
2. System (or teacher) outcome objectives (CELL B)
3. Student process objectives (CELL C)
4. Student outcome objectives (CELL D)

In the systems approach to instructional systems design, we are really only interested in the kind of objectives found in CELL D, student outcome objectives. However, so often we are tempted to write the other kinds, particularly one of the two types of process

```
┌─────────────────────────────────────────────────────┐
│              OBJECTIVE DEVELOPMENT FORM               │
│                                                       │
└─────────────────────────────────────────────────────┘

┌─────────────────────────────────────────────────────┐
│ TOPIC:                                                │
│                                                       │
├───────────────────────────────────────────────────────┤
│ CONDITIONS:                                           │
│                                                       │
│                                                       │
│                                                       │
├───────────────────────────────────────────────────────┤
│ BEHAVIOR:                                             │
│                                                       │
│                                                       │
│                                                       │
│                                                       │
├───────────────────────────────────────────────────────┤
│ CRITERIA:                                             │
│                                                       │
│                                                       │
│                                                       │
│                                                       │
│                                                       │
└─────────────────────────────────────────────────────┘
```

Fig. 4-1

```
                        PROCESS OBJECTIVES   OUTCOME OBJECTIVES
                      ┌─────────────────────┬─────────────────────┐
                      │                     │                     │
 THE INSTRUCTIONAL    │                     │                     │
 SYSTEM               │       CELL A        │       CELL B        │
                      │                     │                     │
                      │                     │                     │
                      ├─────────────────────┼─────────────────────┤
                      │                     │                     │
                      │                     │                     │
 THE STUDENT          │       CELL C        │       CELL D        │
                      │                     │                     │
                      │                     │                     │
                      └─────────────────────┴─────────────────────┘
```

Table 4-1

objectives. I hope this table will help you stay out of trouble.

However, for the purposes of writing CAI lessons, you may find that it is easier and just as functional to skip the writing of objectives altogether and write criterion frames instead.

LESSON DESIGN

Once the elements which will make up the lesson have been represented in some form, it is necessary to turn to the task of designing the overall system and then representing the design in some symbolic manner. This is necessary for planning, communication, and design purposes, as well as for purposes of subsequent revision of the lesson. It is very difficult to make modifications and improvements in a system if you cannot see the overall design of the system. CAI lessons are somewhat unique in this regard. Once the lesson is resident in a computer, you can only see it one frame at a time. It is useful, if not imperative, therefore, to have some sort of overall diagram such as a flow chart.

As we will see in Chapter 7, there are a variety of lesson designs that can be used in the creation of CAI lessons. Using information such as the rationale and learning task analysis, the CAI author must match up the content with the most appropriate design or combination of designs.

System Flow Charts

It is useful to think of flow charts in terms of two levels: **system** flow charts (as discussed here) and **detailed** flow charts (discussed in the following section). A **system** flow chart shows the big picture, but with a small amount of detail. For example, rather lengthy lesson segments made up of many frames but having a single purpose might be represented by a single block on the system flow chart.

The system flow chart is used to represent the major parts of the CAI lesson and to arrange them in the sequence that the lesson will follow. The system flow chart is usually made up of just three types of symbols: the terminator symbol, the operations box, and the decision box.

The terminator symbol is a circle or oval which can be used to represent a starting point, an ending point, or a jump to another specific point in the system flow.

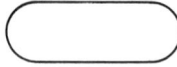

Terminal or Connector Symbol

The operations box is a rectangle (which can be of variable size as required) and represents a segment of the lesson which has a specific, usually singular, purpose.

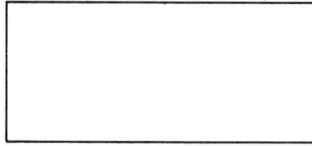

Operations Box

A decision box is a diamond shaped symbol which represents a branching opportunity or choice point in the lesson flow. A decision box is usually used with a single input flow and two possible output points, although it can have three. If a lesson choice point has more than three directions it can go, multiple decision boxes are used in tandem.

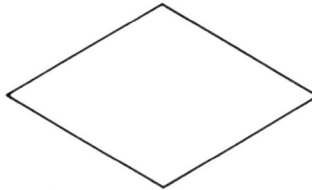

Decision Box

The rules of flow charts are simple (see fig. 4-2). Flow is always shown by arrows pointing down or to the right. Arrows are not allowed to cross each other. Recursive branches (to an earlier point in the program) are shown with terminators.

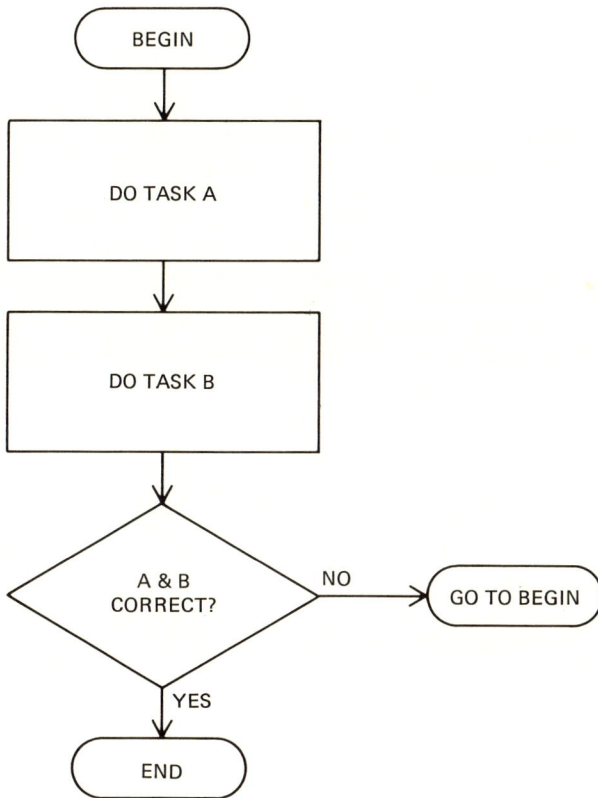

Fig. 4-2

In the system flow chart, there is often a one-to-one relationship between the flow chart elements and the teaching frames as well as the criterion frames. The operations boxes representing a criterion frame, the teaching frames that lead up to it, and the decision box representing the outcome of the student's performance on the criterion frame are shown on the flow chart segment that follows (fig. 4-2)

Detailed Flow Charts

A **detailed** flow chart is much more complete and shows the lesson design right down to the last detail. The system flow chart should be designed first, and, unless the content or the instructional logic of the program is very complicated, there may be no need for a detailed flow chart.

A detailed flow chart can be created by adding detail to the system flow chart, however, a copy of the system flow chart should be retained as it will have continuing utility. A detailed flow chart should show everything, right down to the way each response is judged and all the alternative branches that are taken. The same three symbols will suffice, but feel free to use additional standard flow chart symbols or make up your own.

In practice, almost no one creates a complete detailed flow chart. Usually this degree of specificity is reserved for only those segments of the lesson which are unusually complex.

LESSON CREATION

The lesson creation process is best done in stages as well. For example, if the author is writing criterion frames, it is best to write them for the entire lesson at once, before going on to the next stage of development.

Criterion Frames

In order to know from the beginning exactly the level of learning that the total lesson must produce, it is very useful to write the criterion frames first. At this stage it is easy for another person to see exactly what your CAI lesson is designed to do.

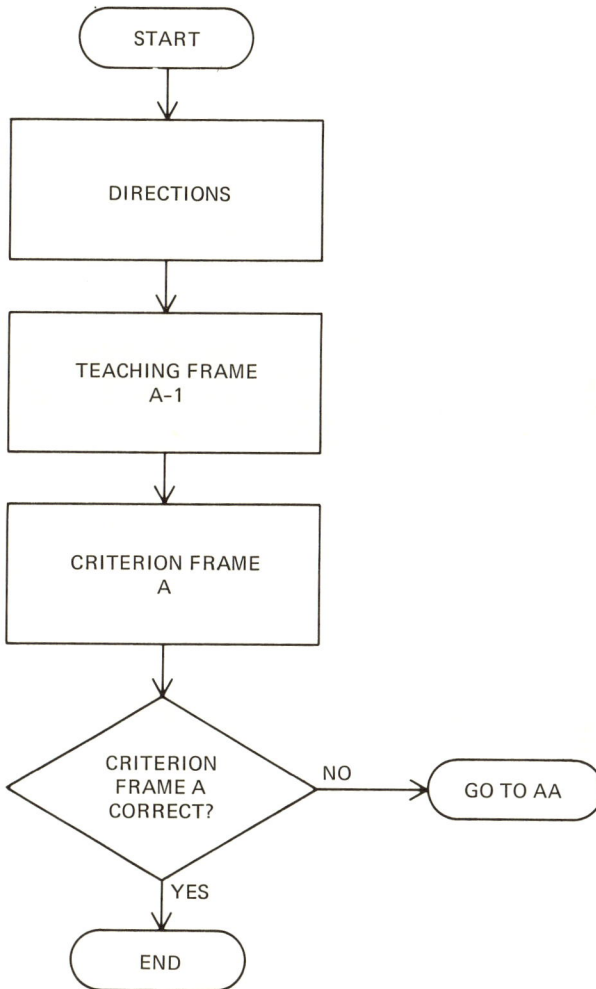

Fig. 4-3

Teaching Frames

The teaching frames, unlike the criterion frames, contain new information and may also contain prompts and cues. A teaching frame may contain a question, or it may consist simply of narrative material.

Teaching frames should be used sparingly, and always in support of the succeeding criterion frame. If caution is not exercised in this regard, it is likely that an unnecessarily "fat" lesson will result. A fat lesson is inefficient and does not use the student's time in a justifiable manner.

Directions

Once all the criterion frames and the teaching frames have been written, and their design as well as the design of the lesson have been determined, it is possible to write the necessary directions to help the student find his or her way through the lesson. Of course, certain minor directions, such as how to respond to a specific frame may be written as the frame, is written. However, the major directions can only be written after the frames are essentially complete.

Lesson Input

Up to this point, the computer need not even be involved in the process. The CAI author would typically have the lesson in script form on paper. Most systems of CAI lesson development include specially made forms for this purpose.

At this point the CAI author should have decided whether he or she will use a CAI authoring system, a CAI author language, or another approach such as a general purpose high-level language like BASIC. If the CAI author has chosen the first option, he or she will simply have to enter the script through the keyboard according to the directions provided. If the author has chosen either of the other two options, he or she will have to create the necessary coding and enter that as well.

Coding

Depending on the language chosen, this will be a more or less difficult and time-consuming step. In either case, the process is essentially the same.

Testing and Debugging

If one of the languages has been used, it is almost certain that considerable "debugging" must be done. The author must test the the program component of the lesson to see that all of the options that the student might legitimately, **or illegitimately,** use work.

LESSON VALIDATION

At this stage of development, the lesson may look complete and ready for distribution, but it is not. It still remains to be proven whether or not the lesson will be effective and efficient in the hands of the users. It is unlikely that **all** your hunches that went into the creation of the lesson are correct. Unfortunately, this is the stage at which most CAI lessons are distributed.

Therefore, it is imperative that your lesson be validated; that is, tested with a group of students who are representative of your intended student population, and then revised until it works properly.

Pretest

In order to ensure that your students are obtaining the required knowledge from the lesson itself and not coming to the lesson already possessing the knowledge, you must create and administer a pretest. The pretest may not be necessary under the conditions within which the lesson will ultimately be used, but it is necessary as part of the validation process. The pretest, like the posttest, should not be a sampling test but should comprehensively screen for all the knowledge that the lesson is designed to impart. Remember, you are not testing the student, you are testing the lesson.

Posttest

The posttest should bear a one-to-one relationship with the pretest. In fact, some authors use the same test. That is probably not a good technique because you cannot tell which improvement is due to the CAI lesson and which is due to the practice effects of the testing.

Field Testing

Field testing should be conducted under conditions which are as realistic as possible. The students should be within the correct age range and at the right stage in their educational program. Some of the field testing data can be collected automatically by the microcomputer, but some of it must be gained the old-fashioned way, by direct observation and hand recording methods. This situation will improve in the future, but the storage capacity of state-of-the-art microcomputers limit what we can do at this point.

Revision

The main purpose of the validation process is to obtain data that will indicate which parts of the lesson need to be improved. It is really at this point that the expertise of the CAI author is tested. In the next chapter, we will get into the issue of lesson "amplification," that is, increasing the power or effectiveness of the lesson.

POSTSCRIPT

There are many advantages to using all of the steps in the systems approach as they are outlined in this chapter. However, it is clearly a very time-consuming process. Therefore, you may want to develop your own modified approach to save you time and yet accomplish the things you want to.

5

INSTRUCTIONAL WRITING AND CAI

Despite the many aids to the CAI authoring process, authoring CAI lessons remains to a very large extent a writing process. All of the content, instructions, questions, responses to questions, and the like are writing tasks.

In many ways instructional writing constitutes a unique form of writing. It is writing with a single-minded purpose — to help another human being understand a concept or fact, retain it, and perhaps use the understanding.

Computer assisted instruction is, in many ways, a very specialized form of instructional writing.

THE RELATIONSHIP BETWEEN WRITING—AS—ART AND INSTRUCTIONAL WRITING

There are those who would argue that "writing is writing" — that all the same rules apply to writing whether it is done in an attempt to create fine literature intended to endure forever, or whether it is for the purpose of leaving a note on the refrigerator door. I do not feel qualified to make general statements about all writing, but I do know that there are many things about instructional or pedagogical writing which are different from some other forms of writing.

One very important difference between instructional writing and artistic writing, for example, is in the use of synonyms for technical terms. In artistic writing the use of synonyms is encouraged, on the grounds that it is creative, adds the spice of variety to writing, and holds the reader's interest. In pedagogical writing, however, the substitution of synonyms for technical terms can introduce confusion that is disastrous.

In poetry, ambiguous and even amphibolous words and phrases are a virtue, adding richness and color. In an instructional passage, ambiguity can destroy learning or worse, produce misunderstanding.

Because much of CAI is merely a specialized form of instructional writing, and because there has been very little emphasis given to this problem, this chapter will explore some of the main characteristics of instructional writing.

DISTRIBUTION OF EMPHASIS

I like to introduce the concept of **distribution of emphasis** with the following story. It seems a man encountered another man crawling around on his hands and knees under a street light. The first man inquired into the problem. The second man said that he had lost his car keys. The first man then said, "That's terrible, I'll help you look." After they had been looking awhile, the first man said, "Exactly what were you doing when you dropped your keys." The second man replied, "I was trying to unlock my car, down the block there." The first man said, "Well then why are you looking here?"

The second man explained simply, "The light's better here."

I think this story has a great deal of relevance for instructional writing. Like the fellow hunting for his keys, we, as instructional writers, are apt to gravitate toward areas that are "well illumined," or easy for us to understand and explain. This is not always the best route, as the story points out. We are also likely to give brief, cursory treatment to those things which are the most difficult for us to understand, and thus we have an uneven distribution of emphasis.

Some facts, concepts, and other things to be learned are simply more difficult to learn than others. The same ones which are most difficult to learn are also likely to be the ones most difficult to write about. In other words, the things the student is apt to have the greatest difficulty with are very likely the same things the instructional writer will find most difficult to write about. The result often is that the instructional writer does a very thorough job of describing the relatively simple things, and gives short shrift to precisely the topics which require a thorough explanation for the student to be able to comprehend them.

Inappropriate distribution of emphasis is one of the most pervasive problems in instructional programs, particularly those that have not undergone conscientious, technically adequate validation.

AMPLIFICATON

Amplification is a term which I have appropriated to refer to the act of increasing the teaching power of a lesson. It consists of working with the various pedagogical devices which are available to increase the instructional effectiveness of a lesson. Recasting, which will be covered next, is one of the primary methods. However, there are others, such as figurative language and mnemonics. These will be covered later in the chapter.

RECASTING

One of the most important skills an instructional writer can have is the ability to recast language. I once met a very memorable college professor. He seemed to have an infinite capacity to restate a concept or fact using different words. He would display this skill hour on end in help sessions he ran voluntarily for undergraduates just before finals each term. His ability to creatively restate — or recast — his lessons was, for his students, a very effective instructional tool.

The ability to recast instructional language is much of what constitutes the art of instructional writing as well as teaching. It is a skill which can be learned and cultivated.

ADVANCE ORGANIZERS

An **advance organizer** refers to material or techniques used in advance of the presentation of the actual lesson content, which is designed to make it easier for the student to relate the new knowledge to knowledge which he already commands. The principle behind advance organizers is that as humans take in new knowledge, they automatically spend considerable mental energy relating it to what they already know. They categorize it, look for inconsistencies, review it for any threatening aspects, and so forth. An advance organizer represents the instructional author's attempt to facilitate this process for the learner, thus saving him or her time and increasing the likelihood of learning and retention.

By learning to use advance organizers, you can greatly increase the effectiveness of your instructional writing. It is possible to go into this topic in much greater depth as there is a sizable body of literature on advance organizers. However, I think it is an obvious enough concept that most people can function quite well intuitively.

To a very real extent, most of an instructional writer's efforts and most of the writing techniques he or she uses, are aimed at relating new knowledge to a students existing store of knowledge.

EXAMPLES

Many times, the best way to amplify a section of a lesson is simply to provide examples. Occasionally, as in the case of discrimination learning, nonexamples are also appropriate.

REPETITION

Sometimes, when one does not feel clever enough to come up with something brilliant, simple repetition will get the job done as well as any thing. There are times when, if a student has missed a question frame, the best thing to do is to give him or her another shot at the frame and perhaps at the frames that lead up to it.

READABILITY LEVEL

One of the most obvious ways to amplify a lesson is to adjust the readability level. If the readability level of a lesson is too high, the passage may not be understood by your target population. If it is at too low a level, your students may become bored, let their minds wander, and not do well on that account. We will now examine several dimensions of readability which can strongly affect the success of your lessons and which you can manage in order to amplify your lessons.

Sentence Length

Short sentences are considered desirable in any form of writing. Instructional writing is very sensitive to sentence length also. In CAI, with the limited microcomputer screen sizes, it is especially crucial. In most formulas for determining reading level, short sentences are associated with lower reading levels and longer sentences with higher reading levels. Similarly, shorter sentences are considered to contribute more to readability than do longer sentences.

Sentence Structure

Sentence structure can be a very salient variable when a segment of a lesson is not teaching. One of the most critical aspects of poor sentence structure is "front-end loading." In a sentence of this kind, the student has to remember too much information from the first (front) part of the sentence before he or she reaches the conclusion — and understands the complete thought — of the sentence. The custom in the English language of putting the adjective before the subject which it modifies automatically contributes to this problem.

Related to this is the faulty question frame in which the blank occurs too early in the frame to allow it to be filled in as it is read. The student must instead read awkwardly past the blank, taking in partial meaning until he or she has read enough of the frame to grasp its meaning and structure a response.

Vocabulary

Vocabulary is a crucial element in instructional writing because of the need to use technical terms in a precise way. As a result, you do not have the same latitude to use synonyms that you do in other forms of writing. Think of the terms connected with the equipment of almost any sport as an example of this principle — they are **golf clubs** — not golf sticks, golf mallets or golf bats.

Of course many of the large words you may be tempted to use **can** be replaced with smaller words. Typically, reducing the size of words and reducing the reading level results in a sizable increase in the word count, or wordiness of the material.

Generally, words with a low frequency of usage in general discourse or general language use (such as magazine writing) are considered to contribute to higher readability levels and vice versa. Technical terms that cannot be avoided, and are in fact part of the content to be learned in an instructional passage, must be considered separately, however, in such calculations.

The problems associated with the use of abbreviations, "buzzwords," and acronyms deserve special mention here. In pedagogical writing it is generally preferable to spell things out rather than use abbreviations. True, it uses more space to do so, but it may actually wind up saving the student time.

There are other features of language, which, while not usually considered by the various formulas for computing readability or grade level, are nonetheless important to the clarity of the written material.

Flow

In straight narrative text the matter of flow is extremely important. It is the writers obligation to be sure that the reader can "follow" the train of thought represented in the material. The reader should not experience any very abrupt or unexpected changes in direction. A CAI lesson presents a very special case in this regard — the screen-by-screen presentation isolates the material and thus increases the possibility that the lesson may not flow. In all lessons it is difficult to scan either forward or backward, and in some, it is impossible.

The best way around this is to build in a lot of of material whose purpose it is to link the various components of the lesson together — that is, nearly every frame should contain words that refer to or are synonyms for information appearing in the previous frames.

This process is made easier if the CAI author creates frames which present only a small amount of new material. Technically, the amount of new material presented in each frame is referred to as **step-size**. In writing PI, it is often the case that step-size is considered to be simply a function of words per frame. This is an unfortunate oversimplification. Sometimes, even a short sentence or frame can represent a very big step — for example, consider the following statement as a frame in a CAI lesson: "Energy is equal to mass times the speed of light squared."

LEANNESS

In instructional writing, it is often better to say less rather than more. There is a cost attached to everything you put into the lesson. For example, each thing the student must read consumes time — time he or she could be applying to something else. Each thing added also adds to the bulk of the lesson, and tends to embed the really important things. In a CAI lesson, there is still another problem — excess material might separate important segments and so weaken the connection that the student might see between them.

Another issue in favor of leanness is the fact that when one is validating material, it may be necessary to add material to a segment which needs to be amplified. There is no logical basis for determining which among several things in a lesson is responsible for the learning. Therefore, it is better to start with a version which is very lean, and plan to add material if it is determined to be necessary by the field test data.

FIGURATIVE LANGUAGE

In artistic writing, figurative language serves the purpose of enriching the writing and entertaining the reader. In instructional writing, figurative language is also a valuable tool. It facilitates the student's learning and recall.

Metaphor

Metaphors can be extremely powerful tools for the amplification of instructional materials. The effective use of metaphor is a measure of the creativity and skill of the instructional writer.

Hyperbole

Oftentimes, a point or perhaps a relationship can be made clearer by means of an exaggeration. Usually, instructional hyperbole is accompanied by a disclaimer, such as, "For didactic purposes only," or, "For purposes of illustration (discussion) only."

OVERSIMPLIFICATION

Many of us learn things easiest if we can first see them in a simplified form, stripped of all "unnecessary" complications. Good instructional writing often includes such a tactic early on, with the necessary details added in gradual steps.

HYPOTHETICAL POINTS

It is sometimes necessary to create hypothetical scenarios in order to facilitate the learning of something perhaps too close to the student for him or her to see it otherwise — a misconception which the student holds which must be given up (or unlearned) before new learning can occur, for example.

INSTRUCTIONAL LOGIC

The constructs of logic comprise an important set of pedagogical tools. These devices are closely related to the way we think and the way we go about proving things to ourselves and to each other. Some of the most commonly used are listed and reviewed here for your reference.

Analogy

I'm sure some wise old person must have said something like the following at one time or another in human history: "We learn the new in the terms of the old." Each student, at every level, comes to the learning situation with a body of personal knowledge and experience so vast that it dwarfs the amount of material to be learned within a given CAI lesson. This wealth of knowledge, much of it in common with the rest of the members of the same culture, can be used as a basis from which to draw analogies.

Much instructional strategy is based upon analogy, in one form or another. Indeed, much writing and human discourse in general is based upon analogy. The thing that makes instructional writing different from other writing, at least in so far as it involves analogies, is the **extent** to which it draws analogies.

Syllogism

One very special way of helping a student to relate new knowledge to existing knowledge is by using syllogisms. The use of a syllogism exploits the student's prior knowledge base in a more specific way than does an analogy. The syllogism usually draws on the fact that a given class of objects to be learned has properties in common. If the instructional author points out to the student that an object under study is a member of such a class, the student can draw on his previous knowledge of that class of objects to reach concliusions about the object under study.

Syllogisms are also a good basis for the construction of question frames. For example, if a medical student is introduced to a new disease, and the instructional treatment includes the fact that it is a **contagious** disease, then frames can be used which cause the student to draw conclusions about some sort of process by which the disease is transmitted from one victim to another.

CREDIBILITY AND PROOF

There is a strong relationship between the credibility which a student can place in material and the likelihood that it will be understood and remembered. There are several bases that instructional writers can use to establish credibility in their lessons.

Authority

One of the most common ways of establishing the credibility of materials is to rely on the authority of an expert or perhaps an organization the student is likely to know and respect. The simplest way to do this is merely to state the relationship between the source of authority and the material.

Rational Argument as Proof

One of the oldest techniques in scholarship is to construct logical arguments which are likely to be compelling to the student — in other words, to use reasoning power to convince the student that the material is valid and true. Prior to the rise of empiricism and the scientific method, rational argument was the primary tool of scholarship. Although the rational approach has fallen from favor somewhat (in academia at least), it still remains the best way to deal with material for which there is no empirical data.

Empirical Proof

The premier way to convince students of the validity of your material is to cite empircal proof. We live in an empirical age, when great credance is given to "seeing the hard evidence." When it is possible, you should provide such evidence in support of your lessons.

LISTS

Placing items in lists often makes it easier to see relationships between them. In addition to simple lists, it is possible to use lists which show hierarchical relationships between things by using rubrics of different levels. However, when there is no hierarchical relationship or even serial relationship between the elements of a list, you may want to avoid the use of numbers in order not to imply that there is.

MANAGEMENT OF WHITE SPACE

The skillful use of of page (or screen) layout, sometimes called the management of white space, can produce economies in your materials. For example, if there are patterns that repeat in material, you can avoid having to label and explain a lot of things by having elements which have the same function always appear in the same place on the page or display.

GRAPHIC ILLUSTRATION

Many of the microcomputers available are quite capable with graphics. It is part of the writer's responsibility to recognize when the material can benefit from graphic representation and to either design it or seek assistance with designing it. There is no doubt some truth to the aphorism "One picture is worth a thousand words," even in instructional writing.
While illustrations are not writing as such, the specification of them, or the development of "story-boards," is. Furthermore, the graphics must support and enhance the written portion of the lesson. Therefore, it is part of the writer's responsibility to determine the use of graphics.

MNEMONICS

In the context of CAI authorship, a mnemonic device is anything which makes the material more memorable. It is unfortunate that for many teachers and instructional writers, **mnemonics** is a dirty word. Many seem to feel that if they have to "resort" to the use of a mnemonic device, their "real" techniques have failed.

In the CAI field, the ability to create good mnemonic devices is an important stock in trade. A good mnemonic device can save an awful lot of programming effort, since it can largely eliminate the need to provide the student with practice on many topics.

Acronyms

One of the most effective mnemonic devices is the acronym. It allows the student to remember a list of related things, if they can be arranged in a sequence that permits their initial letters to spell out a recognizable word, or even a a characteristic pattern. Watch for the opportunity to create acronyms.

Alliteration

When two or more items must be remembered each of which begins with the same letter, you can capitalize on the fact by calling the student's attention to it and thus facilitating retention of the information. Sometimes you can help the process along by using synonyms for one or more of the terms.

Aphorisms

The history of human learning and socialization is replete with aphorisms. They can be a valuable learning tool in CAI, as well. One pair of aphorisms from the first-aid training field provides a good example of the effectiveness of aphorisms: "When the face is pale, raise the tail" and "When the face is red, raise the head."

CAVEATS

My usual approach, and one which I have tried to follow in writing this book, is to discuss things in positive terms — to emphasize what should be done rather than what shouldn't be done. However, just briefly, I would like to depart from that posture and include some "shouldn'ts."

Ambiguity and Amphiboly

The terms **ambiguity** and **amphiboly** are related in an interesting way, of which most people are unaware. The term ambiguity refers to a situation in which a **single word** has two or more meanings. When two or more words, such as a phrase or sentence, have two or more meanings, they are said to be amphibolous. I mention this because both types of error crop up frequently — particularly in material which has been greatly simplified, as in the case of material written for children. It is my hope that it will be helpful to you to know the difference so that you may more easily spot these errors and eliminate them from the lessons you write.

Vagueness

Beware of the tendency to substitute vagueness for clarity in your materials. One is sometimes tempted to do this on the most difficult material, the very material with which the student is also likely to have the most difficulty.

Inconsistent Use of Technical Terms

Much instructional material consists of teaching the student the proper meaning of technical terms and how to use them. Don't make it any more difficult for the student than it has to be by using technical terms casually.

SUMMARY

In many ways, CAI authorship is merely a specialized form of writing. The extent to which the specialized nature of the writing is observed will have a lot to do with the success of your CAI lessons, perhaps more than any other factor including the way in which the computer is used.

6

CAI FRAME PROTOCOLS

The story (perhaps apochryphal) is told of one of the pioneers in the programmed instruction movement. It was at the time when the term **frame** was just coming into use as a name for the smallest unit of the PI lesson. It seems a company wrote to this pioneer asking for a quotation on a project to write twelve hundred frames of

PI. Our pioneer wrote back a simple letter which said, "What's a frame?" The flustered company representive wrote back, giving a thorough definition of the term "frame."   The pioneer then had a staff member calculate the average number of "frames" in a yard of the paper scroll that was used on the teaching machine they wrote for. He then sent a bid offering to write **x** yards of programmed instruction for **y** dollars.

WHAT'S A FRAME?

As the story illustrates, **Frame** is a **conventional** term that has come to mean the amount of information that is presented on the microcomputer display screen at any one time. A frame may contain straight narrative text or it may contain a question, or a combination of both. The concept of a **frame** is useful as an indexing tool — a way of referring to a specific part of a CAI lesson, or as one unit of measure of lesson size. Synonyms for the term **frame** would be **display, screen,** or even **CRT.** Some CAI authoring systems have their own terminolgy and use **page** as an equivalent term. I prefer **frame.**

WHAT'S A FRAME PROTOCOL?

A **frame protocol** is basically a **sample frame** that is so typical of a class of frame type that it can serve as a model for the design of other frames. This chapter contains a number of frame protocols that may help you to enlarge your repertoire of frame types which you are capable of using. One of the strengths of good CAI lessons is a variety of well-chosen frame types. The variety itself is important, of course, because it makes the program more interesting. However, the real benefit of having a large repertoire of frame types is that you are better able to select optimum frame types for specific learning events.
We will first look at some interesting categories of frame-types. Then we will look at a series of frame protocols, considering various properties of good frames as we go.

FRAME TYPES

Frames can be thought of as being in two major categories — teaching frames and criterion frames. Maintaining the distinction can be very helpful in the planning, production, and revision or validation of CAI lessons.

A **teaching frame** is one which contains information for the student to learn. Often, it contains enough information so that the student could answer the frame without seeing any other frames in the lesson. A teaching frame may or may not require a response. For example, figure 6-1 is an example of a teaching frame.

IT IS CUSTOMARILY CONSIDERED SAFE TO

EAT OYSTERS ONLY IN MONTHS CONTAINING

THE LETTER "R".

Fig. 6-1   A teaching frame which requires no response

A frame such as that shown in figure 6-1 which requires no response is also called a **presentation frame.** This kind of frame is very useful and quite valid.

Teaching frames which contain questions are perhaps even more common. Typically, the teaching frame will also contain all the information which is necessary to answer that question (see fig. 6-2).

```
ALL TREES WHICH LOSE THEIR LEAVES IN WINTER

ARE CALLED DECIDUOUS TREES.

A MAPLE TREE LOSES ITS LEAVES IN WINTER.

IS THE MAPLE TREE A DECIDUOUS TREE?

ANSWER Y OR N.
```

Fig. 6-2 A teaching frame which requires a response

It is obvious in figure 6-2 that the student could answer this frame without looking at any other part of the lesson.
Sometimes a teaching frame containing a question is so obvious that it requires almost no thought or problem solving at all. Some frames of this type are so obvious that they are called "copy" frames (see fig. 6-3).

```
THIS IS A USEFUL SPELLING RULE:

I BEFORE E EXCEPT IN WORDS WHICH RHYME WITH

WAY, SUCH AS NEIGHBOR AND WEIGH.

TYPE THE WORD SLEIGH IN THE SPACE BELOW.

    _____
```

Fig. 6-3 A question frame which is so simple
it is called a "copy" frame

The term **copy frame** is often used in a pejorative way to describe a frame which is unintentionally so simple that it accomplishes no pedagogical purpose. Many copy frames deserve this criticism, particularly when it is clear that the author should not have used such a frame under the circumstances. However, there are times when a copy frame is quite appropriate. For example, the first time a technical term is introduced, or, perhaps in a spelling drill-and-practice program.

A **criterion frame** is one in which absolutely no teaching is intended to take place. That is, it is devoid of hints, clues, or any other information which would "give away" the answer. Figure 6-4 is an example of a criterion frame.

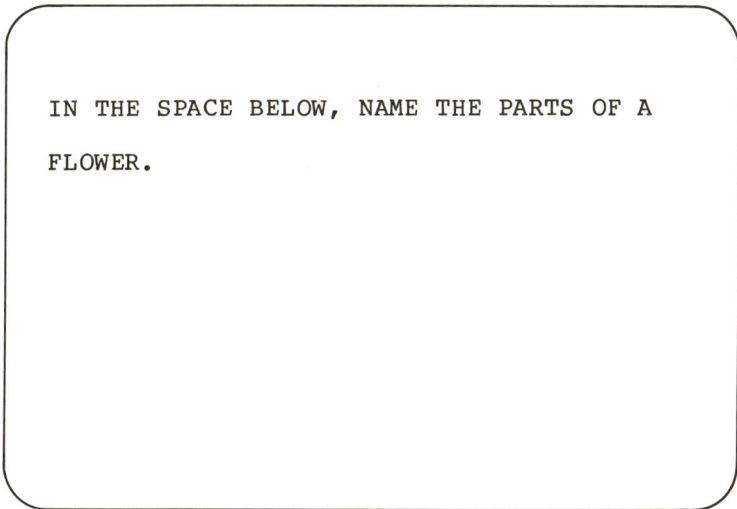

```
┌──────────────────────────────────────────────┐
│                                                │
│   IN THE SPACE BELOW, NAME THE PARTS OF A      │
│                                                │
│   FLOWER.                                      │
│                                                │
│                                                │
│                                                │
│                                                │
│                                                │
│                                                │
└──────────────────────────────────────────────┘
```

Fig. 6-4   A criterion frame

The concept of a criterion frame is a very useful one. Criterion frames basically measure whether or not your students have met the learning "criterion." Criterion frames are also the main device by which the CAI author can determine the effectiveness of the sequence of the lesson to which the criterion frame refers.

It is common practice to begin the construction of a lesson by writing all of the criterion frames first. The author then writes only enough teaching frames, in front of each of the criterion frames, to enable the student to answer each of the criterion frames correctly.

FRAME PROTOCOLS

The frame protocols that will be presented here are not meant to be an exhaustive set. There are no doubt many other protocols that could have been included. Undoubtedly, you will invent other types and you will encounter other types in the flood of CAI which is now being written and will appear over the next few years.

However, it is hoped that this chapter will enlarge your repertoire of available frame types and that you will use this chapter as a reference to enrich your programs with variety. It is also hoped that you will learn some of the principles of good frame designs and avoid some errors in your work. Further, you will learn to think in terms of the concept of frame protocols and will continue to add to your repertoire of frame types by expanding this collection of protocols.

The protocols that follow are arranged in categories which are not perfect categories. There is some overlap, because all of the categories are not mutually exclusive. However, the main purpose of illustrating the underlying concepts is achieved, I think.

ALTERNATIVE RESPONSE FRAMES

Alternative response frames describes a broad category of frame formats for questions in which the student must select the correct answer from among a set of possible "alternatives," all of which are explicitly provided on the screen. Alternative response frames are in contradistinction to constructed response frames, which will be discussed in the next section.

Two-Way-Choice Frames

Two-way-choice frames are widely used. Perhaps it is because they are nearly the simplest way to ascertain if a student has learned something, without introducing a lot of extraneous information as distractors. Or, perhaps it is because a lot of things to be learned involve two-way choices. At any rate they are useful frames which are easy to write and do the job efficiently.

72

```
IF AN OPERATOR PLACES A CALL FOR YOU AND

YOUR CALL CANNOT BE COMPLETED, YOU WILL

BE CHARGED A SMALL SERVICE FEE ANYWAY.


TYPE Y OR N.
```

Fig. 6-5 A two-way-choice alternative response frame

The most commonly used types of two-way-choice frames are   true or false (usually given as T or F) and yes or no (usually given as Y or N) frames (see fig. 6-5). These items work well for a great many purposes.

Check Frames

Check frames are a unique type of two way choice frame (see fig. 6-6).

```
IF THE RATCHET PAWL IS RELEASED, THE

MAIN TYPE-ACTION CAM WILL ROTATE

( A. CLOCKWISE/ B. COUNTERCLOCKWISE )

UNTIL THE RATCHET PAWL AGAIN ENGAGES.
```

Fig. 6-6 A special two-way-choice frame called
a check frame or a tick frame

A check frame, or tick frame, is so called because
in its original setting, in paper-and-pencil programmed
instruction, it called for the student to put a "check"
mark or "tick" mark by his or her choice. It was a
useful, response-economic mode which saved the student
time. The check frame can be very good when used with a
light pen.

Two-way-choice frames such as those described above
provide an efficient way to give students practice with
the material and to check their understanding. In
addition, two-way-choice items can be used to provide
students an opportunity to make judgments about and
influence the course of their own learning (fig. 6-7)

```
DO YOU FEEL THAT YOU HAVE SUFFICIENT

UNDERSTANDING OF THE GROSS ANATOMY OF THE

SPLEEN TO MOVE ON TO MICROANATOMY?

Y OR N?
```

Fig. 6-7 A two-way-choice frame that solicits
the student's judgment about whether to move on

Multiple-Choice Frames

Another very common type of frame is the multiple-
choice item (see fig. 6-8).

```
BASSWOOD IS TECHNICALLY CLASSIFIED AS

HARDWOOD, EVEN THOUGH IT IS VERY SOFT,

BECAUSE

        A.  IT IS 1.7 ON THE HARDNESS SCALE.

        B.  IT IS HARD WHEN FRESHLY CUT.

        C.  IT LOSES ITS LEAVES IN WINTER.

        D.  IT IS HARD TO FIND.

TYPE THE LETTER OF YOUR ANSWER HERE:
```

Fig. 6-8 A multiple-choice frame

The first part of this type of item is called the **stem**. The choices are usually called **foils**. Usually just one of the foils is correct and the others are incorrect, provided as **distractors** to test the student's ability to choose the correct answer.

There are many variations of the multiple-choice frame. For example, although four foils is probably the most common type, there is no reason to have as many as four or to limit the number to four. It is usually the case that only one of the foils is correct; however, feel free to have none, all, or any number in between correct. In this mannner you can strengthen your items and make them more flexible.

BABOON Frames

BABOON is an acronym for B, A, BO(th), O(r) N(either). It is a special class of multiple-choice frame that has certain distinct advantages (see fig. 6-9).

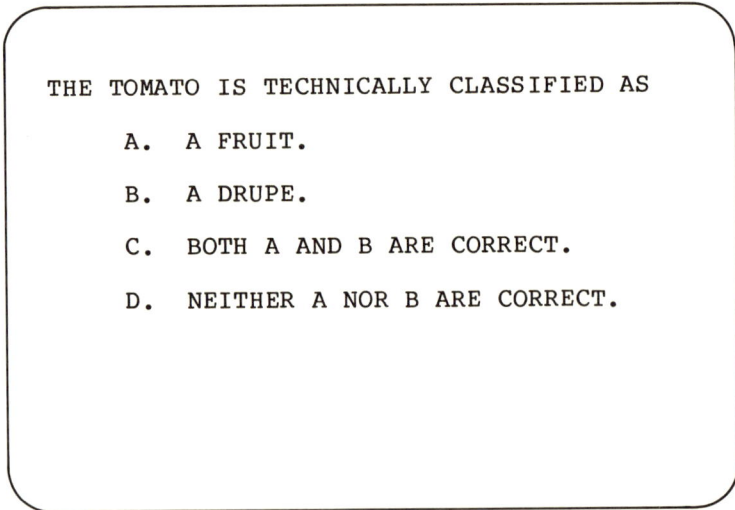

THE TOMATO IS TECHNICALLY CLASSIFIED AS

    A.   A FRUIT.

    B.   A DRUPE.

    C.   BOTH A AND B ARE CORRECT.

    D.   NEITHER A NOR B ARE CORRECT.

Fig. 6-9   A BABOON frame

The main advantage of a BABOON frame is the relative freedom from prompting. Therefore, it is quite a useful format for a criterion frame. It is also a somewhat easier frame to write, since it has the advantages of a multiple-choice frame without the work involved in thinking up so many distractors.

Matching Frames

Matching frames are a variation on the theme of multiple- choice items. They are useful because they can elicit a lot of student participation in a small amount of time and space (see fig. 6-10).

```
MATCH THE ITEM ON THE LEFT WITH THE ITEM ON
THE RIGHT BY TYPING ITS NUMBER IN THE
CORRECT SPACE.

1 H2O              _ COMMON SALT

2 NACL             _ HYDROCHLORIC ACID

3 HCL              _ CARBON DIOXIDE

4 CO2              _ AMMONIA

5 CO               _ WATER

6 NAOH             _ CARBON MONOXIDE
```

Fig. 6-10   A matching frame

CONSTRUCTED RESPONSE FRAMES

Constructed response items are so called because the student is asked to create or "construct" the answer, rather than to choose it from among alternative responses provided.

Fill-in-the-Blank Frames

The most common type of constructed response item requires the student to fill in one or more blanks within a sentence as in fig. 6-11.

```
┌─────────────────────────────────────────────────────────────┐
│                                                               │
│   SINCE THE LONGER LIGHT WAVES ARE TOWARD THE                 │
│                                                               │
│   RED END OF THE SPECTRUM, IT FOLLOWS THAT                    │
│                                                               │
│   THE SHORTER LIGHT WAVES ARE TOWARD THE                      │
│                                                               │
│   _____ END OF THE SPECTRUM.                      │
│                                                               │
│                                                               │
│                                                               │
│                                                               │
│                                                               │
│                                                               │
└─────────────────────────────────────────────────────────────┘
```

Fig. 6-11   A fill-in-the-blank frame

Mechanically, there are several ways to handle this. The author might move the cursor (the spot of light which indicates the screen position at which the computer is prepared to display the next character entered) to the first location of the blank for the convenience of the student. A second way is to direct the student to construct the response at the bottom of the screen rather than within the blank. A space may be indicated at the bottom of the screen for this, or it may simply be left blank, since it really doesn't matter exactly where the answer appears on the screen.

Another type of constructed response item is the sentence completion format. This format is not so commonly used, but it works quite nicely. The cursor can simply be left at the end of the incomplete sentence, at the point where the student should begin the response which will complete the sentence. A good program will find and evaluate the student's response no matter where it is located on the screen.

A third type of constructed response includes those items which require that the student calculate and supply an answer. This type of item often occurs in arithmetic lessons and the like.

Constructed responses are typically more difficult to evaluate than alternative responses since students have much less structure to guide them in making an answer. Constructed responses are much more variable. However, the freedom afforded the student may be precisely the strength of constructed response items.

Sentence Completion Frame

Sentence completion frames are not used a great deal because their open-endedness tends to elicit student responses which are difficult to judge. However, if you are in an early developmental phase and you are able to observe student responses carefully, a sentence completion frame can give you a lot of information about possible student responses very quickly. Such a frame can also be appropriate when the response tendency has been well strengthened, particularly when the response sought is a specific technical term. At any rate the open-ended sentence completion frame is best reserved for necessary use — for example, as a criterion frame (see fig. 6-12).

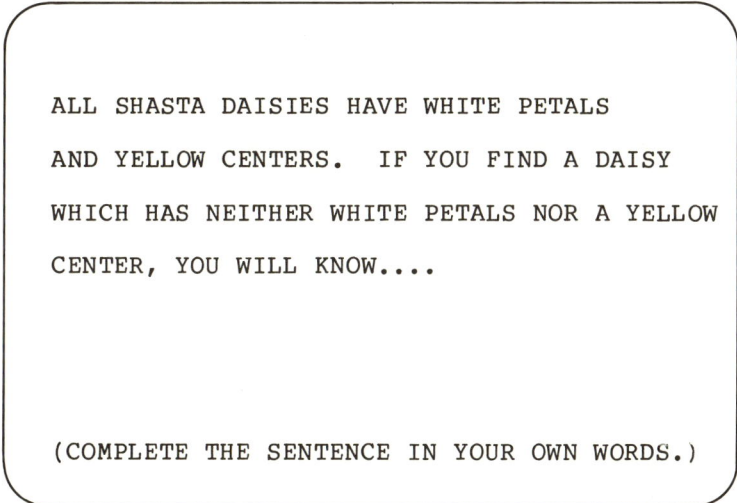

```
ALL SHASTA DAISIES HAVE WHITE PETALS

AND YELLOW CENTERS.  IF YOU FIND A DAISY

WHICH HAS NEITHER WHITE PETALS NOR A YELLOW

CENTER, YOU WILL KNOW....




(COMPLETE THE SENTENCE IN YOUR OWN WORDS.)
```

Fig. 6-12 A sentence-completion frame

In your response judging, you should look for some sign of negation such as the words **not, no,** or perhaps just the letter **n.** You should also look carefully for the term **Shasta daisy.** You will not want to accept just **daisy,** without the term **Shasta.**

Short-Answer Frames

Short answer frames are used frequently in mathematical lessons, and they can work quite well in verbal, tutorial CAI as well (see fig. 6-13).

```
THE CREW OF THE WINNING BOAT IN THE 1980

AMERICA'S CUP RACE WERE AGED 46 YEARS, 32

YEARS, 24 YEARS, AND 19 YEARS.


WHAT WAS THE AVERAGE AGE OF THE CREW?
```

Fig. 6-13   A short-answer frame

Short-answer frames are deceptively difficult to use. They put a strong demand on the author to write the question in such a way that the answer options are sufficiently restricted. Otherwise, the response will be much too hard for the computer to judge properly. If the author does not handle the answer shaping properly in the question frame or in the material which goes before it, the burden simply shifts to the response-judging phase.

THE LOGIC OF FRAMES

Some of the most powerful devices that you can use in the design of frames are the constructs of formal logic. They structure your thinking as an author and they give the student experience in thinking logically as they exercise him in the content he or she is to learn.

Syllogism

The syllogism forms the logical basis for many good frames (see fig. 6-14).

```
┌─────────────────────────────────────────────────────────┐
│  LARGE COMPUTERS, MADE UP OF MANY DISCRETE                │
│  ELECTRONIC COMPONENTS PRODUCE MORE HEAT AND              │
│  THEREFORE REQUIRE MORE AIR CONDITIONING                  │
│  THAN COMPUTERS MADE WITH INTEGRATED                      │
│  CIRCUITS.                                                │
│  THE Z1000 IS A LARGE COMPUTER MADE WITH                  │
│  DISCRETE ELECTRONIC COMPONENTS.                          │
│  THEREFORE THE Z1000 ([] WILL/[] WILL NOT)               │
│  REQUIRE MUCH AIR CONDITIONING.                           │
└─────────────────────────────────────────────────────────┘
```

Fig. 6-14 A syllogism-based frame

Both alternative response frames and constructed response frames can be based on a syllogism.   The frame above would be a good frame to use with a light pen.

Discrimination Learning

Discrimination learning involves learning to tell the **difference** between things. Frames using this logic often take the form of multiple-choice frames. The important thing is the relationship between the frame logic and the ultimate use to which the student will put the learning.

Generalization Learning

A frame whose logic involves generalization learning requires the student to identify the **similarities** among things.

Deduction

Frames based on the logic of deduction require the student to use a set of facts to deduce a conclusion. A deduction frame takes the form: If A, then B, C, and D.

Induction

Frames based on the logic of induction require that the student reason inductively to reach a conclusion. In general, it means that the student will learn to look at a lot of isolated facts and reach a conclusion about something they all have in common.

Analogy

A frame which uses an analogy, usually between something students already know and the thing which they are to learn about, can be very effective. In a frame using an analogy, it is important that students realize that the two things are not identical, and that the similarity is being used for didactic purposes only.

Metaphor

Frames using metaphors can be especially effective, since they often create rich imagery which the student can use as a mnemonic device to enhance retention and recall. In a metaphor the thing to be learned is treated as if it actually was some other, more common entity with which the student is already familiar.

EGRUL Frames

EGRUL and RULEG frames should be considered as a mutually exclusive pair of categories. EG stands for e.g., or example. RUL simply stands for rule. An EGRUL frame is one in which the logic flows from the examples to the rule covering the examples. Conversely, a RULEG frame is one in which the logic flows from the rule to the examples. The frame that follows is an EGRUL frame (fig. 6-15).

```
┌─────────────────────────────────────────────┐
│                                               │
│   WHAT DO THE FOLLOWING PERSONS HAVE IN       │
│                                               │
│   COMMON?                                      │
│                                               │
│   ABRAHAM LINCOLN                              │
│                                               │
│   WILLIAM MCKINLEY                             │
│                                               │
│   JOHN KENNEDY                                 │
│                                               │
│   THEY WERE ALL PRESIDENTS WHO WERE            │
│                                               │
│   _____ IN OFFICE.       │
│                                               │
│                                               │
└─────────────────────────────────────────────┘
```

Fig. 6-15   An EGRUL frame

The exemplars here are persons who have something in common that sets them apart from any other set of persons. The rule, or thing they have in common, is that all three were assassinated while holding the office of president of the United States.

RULEG Frames

RULEG frames are just the inverse of EGRUL frames. The student is given the rule and must then think of examples (see fig. 6-16).

```
A BIVALVE MOLLUSK HAS TWO HARD, CONCAVE,

SHELL HALVES HINGED TO EACH OTHER AT ONE

SIDE, ENCLOSING A FLESHY BODY.  WHICH OF

FOLLOWING ARE MOLLUSKS?

A. AN OYSTER      D. A QUAHOG

B. A LIMPET       E. A BARNACLE

C. A MUSSEL       F. A SEA URCHIN

TYPE THE LETTER(S) OF YOUR ANSWER(S)
HERE:
```

Fig. 6-16   A RULEG frame

In a RULEG frame the student is usually required to apply a rule to some examples affected by the rule, or sometimes to generate examples to fit the rule.

PROMPTS

Prompts can be thought of as aids that the CAI author builds in to help the student develop the answer to the questions in the lesson. Some prompts are obviously better than others. In general, a prompt that helps the student to understand the material being taught is preferred to one that does not.

Prompts can be thought of as being one of two kinds _ formal prompts or thematic prompts. Formal prompts are so called because they rely on "form" of various aspects of the frame for their effectiveness. Thematic prompts are so called because they refer to the "theme" of the material for their effect. Formal prompts may depend on such things as the number of letters in an answer. Thematic prompts call on the student to understand and use the meaning of the material to produce answers.

Formal Prompts

The following frame illustrates the use of formal prompts (fig 6-17).

```
THE CARVED AND PAINTED EFFIGY FOUND AT THE

BOW OF SOME SHIPS IS CALLED A F_____ H___.

THE MAST HEAD IS FOUND AT THE TOP (HEAD) OF

THE M___.
```

Fig. 6-17   A frame containing strong formal prompts

This frame contains strong formal prompts in the form of initial letters and dashes showing the number of letters to be filled in. These are common formal prompts, but there are others. For example, the length of blanks can be used to indicate the length of word that is required, or the number of blanks can be used to indicate the number of words. Another technique is rhyme, as in "rhymes with." The game of charades often uses a number of formal prompts.

Thematic Prompts

Generally speaking, thematic prompts are preferred to formal prompts. Thematic prompts provide more evidence that the student has provided an answer for the right reason. A student can often provide an answer based on a strong formal prompt and not understand why the answer is correct. The following frame illustrates the use of a thematic prompt (fig. 6-18).

```
AN IMMIGRANT IS SOMEONE WHO HAS MOVED FROM

ANOTHER COUNTRY AND PLANS TO MAKE THE NEW

COUNTRY HIS PERMANENT HOME.

LITTLE LARS MOVED FROM NORWAY TO THE U.S.

WITH HIS PARENTS, AND THEY PLAN TO STAY IN

THE U.S. FOREVER.  LARS AND HIS FAMILY ARE

_____S TO THE U.S.
```

Fig. 6-18   A frame which uses a strong thematic prompt

In figure 6-18, it is clear that the student would have to understand the theme of the frame, that is the significance of the term **immigrant,** in order to answer the frame. Note that there are also two formal prompts as well, but they are not enough to stimulate the anwswer by themselves, without the help of the thematic prompt. The formal prompts are, of course, the size of the blank and the letters immediately following the blank.

The Fading of Prompts

The secret of using prompts effectively and yet not overprompting, is to use them liberally in the beginning of a lesson sequence and then to use them more sparingly as you go along, so that by the time you reach the end of the lesson sequence, they play no role at all. This process is called "fading the prompts" or "prompt fading" as you prefer. Prompt fading will be covered in greater detail in the chapter on CAI lesson design. It is mentioned here to underscore the importance of being able to write a variety of different frame styles, including those which have no prompts and those which have prompts of all different strengths.

CHARACTERISTICS OF GOOD FRAMES

Writing CAI lessons is hard, time-consuming work, even for those of us who enjoy it. Therefore, there is a tendency not to examine frames we have written too closely, particularly if they "look" right and seem to work reasonably well. However, there are some common-sense ideas we can follow which will help our programs to work better and to be better accepted by students.

Response Economy

Students can be asked to make many different types of responses. For example, they can be asked simply to read something. They can be asked to construct a response by keying words in. Or they can be asked to key in a single symbol, standing for the answer they have chosen. Alternatively, if the microcomputer is appropriately equipped, they can be asked to point to the chosen response with a "light pen." On a system equipped with voice recognition, they might only have to speak the response.

You can see that all of the response modes listed above call for varying amounts of response effort from the student. This might seem like a minor distinction when considered in the abstract. However, when this difference is magnified over the length of a CAI lesson which is several hours long, it can add up to a lot of time. Therefore, when there is no good pedagogical reason to do otherwise, opt for the most economical response mode.

```
LIST THE FIVE LARGEST CITIES IN THE U.S.

    1. _____

    2. _____

    3. _____

    4. _____

    5. _____
```

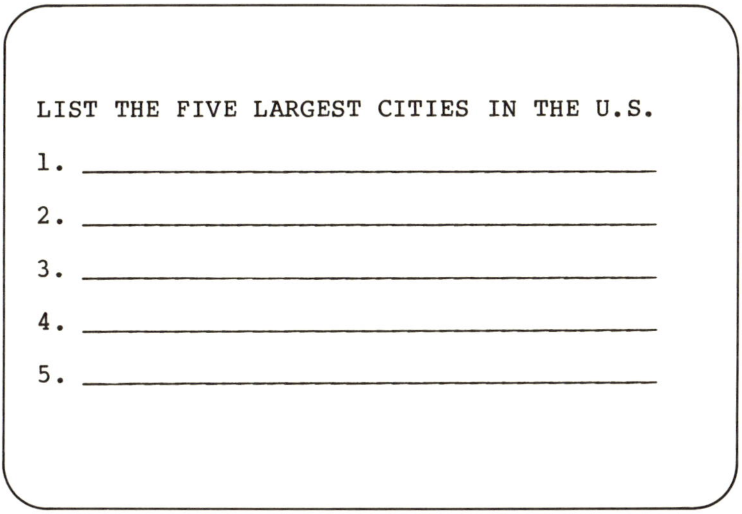

Fig. 6-19 A criterion frame
with a very uneconomical response mode

In figure 6-19 a great many key strokes are required. It may be that they serve a valid pedagogical purpose. If they do not, it is a terrible waste of a student's time. The frame might have been written as follows (see fig. 6-20) and still serve some of the same purposes.

```
WHICH OF THE FOLLOWING CITIES IS NOT AMONG

THE FIVE LARGEST CITIES IN THE U.S.?

A. HOUSTON          E. LOS ANGELES

B. CHICAGO          F. BOSTON

C. PHILADELPHIA     G. MIAMI

D. NEW YORK         H. PHOENIX

LIST THE LETTERS OF YOUR ANSWERS BELOW:
```

Fig. 6-20   A criterion frame
with a more economical response mode

While it is clear that the frame in figure 6-20 does not do exactly what the frame in figure 6-19 does, it might still accomplish what is required within its instructional context, and with more response economy. This example is merely intended to show the kinds of instructional design decisions you must be prepared to make.

Response Relevance

A major consideration — even more important than response economy — is response relevance. Does the response relate well to what the lesson is training the student for? Is it the same kind of response the student will be expected to make when he or she is finished with the lesson? If it is a criterion frame, does it really test the relevant criterion? It is one of the oldest, and dirtiest tricks in pedagogy to teach one thing and test for another.

A common problem in poorly written, inneffective CAI occurs when authors require a response that simply is trivial (fig. 6-21).

88

```
┌─────────────────────────────────────────────┐
│                                               │
│  GENERAL NAPOLEON BONAPARTE WON MANY BATTLES  │
│                                               │
│  BEFORE HE LOST THE ONE BATTLE AT WATERLOO.   │
│                                               │
│  NAME ANY TWO OF THOSE BATTLES.               │
│                                               │
│  1. _____  │
│                                               │
│  2. _____  │
│                                               │
│                                               │
│                                               │
└─────────────────────────────────────────────┘
```

Fig. 6-21 A criterion frame
with a trivial response required

Obviously, whether a response is trivial or not depends
on many things, such as the instructional context and the
objectives of the instruction. In the case of the frame
in figure 6-21, the importance of the response might
depend on whether you were a descendent of Napoleon or
not.

Step Size

Step size is another conventional term. It has come
to be used as the unit of measure for the size of a
frame. Step size refers to the size of the step or
portion of the program content that the frame covers. As
you will see, this is not an unambiguous term — it has
many possible meanings.

The most common meaning of step size is the
physical size of the frame in words. This can be a very
misleading measure, since a frame made up of very few
words can be so abstract that it is difficult and time-
consuming for the student to understand the meaning. It
is well known to readability experts that clear writing
is often very wordy. A frame that is wordy, but clear,
would be much faster to read and comprehend than a short
frame, the meaning of which was abstract and obscure.

Similarly, a frame could contain a question which
was very short but which was not led up to by an
effective teaching sequence. This frame could take a
very long time for the student to accomplish, and we
would have to conclude that even though it was a short

frame in terms of words, it was in fact a big frame, and a large step.

Therefore, another, and perhaps better, meaning of step size is the average length of time it takes for students to complete the frame. This is, of course, a more difficult measure to use since, unlike word count which can be used without actually implementing the lesson, you must field-test the lesson with representative students to determine step size as a function of time to accomplish the frame.

In fact, the measure of step size used most often is simply the subjective judgment of the CAI author. This method may not be as empirical or as mathematically precise as the other methods, but it does permit a great many factors, such as the author's possible experience with the potential students, to be integrated.

Some Miscellaneous Factors Affecting Frame Quality

One of the most common, and most unforgivable, problems in CAI courseware is misspelling. It is especially unforgivable because it is so easy to edit material on a microcomputer and correct spelling errors. At the very least you should have a friend — who makes different spelling errors than you do — go over your material for errors. The big problem with spelling errors is that they undermine the credibility of your courseware. The students then lose respect for the lesson, and so will have difficulty learning from it and, particularly, retaining what they have learned.

In the case of fill-in-the-blank frames, the blank should come as near the end of the frame as possible — how can the student fill in the blank until he or she has read the frame? Putting the blank too early in the frame can make the frame very awkward and slow to accomplish.

AMPLIFICATION OF FRAMES

What do you do with frames which your field testing prove to be ineffective? There are many options, but which should you choose? You can rewrite the frame. You can split it into two or more frames. The general term that I prefer for this process of magnifying or increasing the power of the frames is amplification.

RELATIONSHIPS AMONG FRAMES

The relationships among frames is an important issue which has a lot to do with the effectiveness of frames and how they are written. In order for the student to feel that the program flows smoothly and logically, each frame should contain some reference to frames that have gone before and perhaps those that will come after. It is also very helpful to include brief summaries at certain intervals in the program, as well as frames which foreshadow what is to follow.

The effectiveness of any frame is only partly a function of what is contained within it. The context within which it exists, and the frames which have come before it, in particular, have great effect on the way a frame works; but then that is the concern of later chapters.

CAI LESSON DESIGNS

THE ROLE OF DESIGN IN CAI LESSONS

Architects have an expression: "We shape our buildings, thereafter the buildings shape us." The same aphorism applies to most aspects of computers, including the design of CAI lessons. If you do not start out with a solid, appropriate design, the effectiveness of the lesson will be minimal at best, and revision will be difficult if not impossible.

The designs described here are classic designs which have evolved from CAI practice with large computers. They do not represent all of the designs which have been used, and certainly they do not represent all of the designs which will eventually be used. Indeed, one of the most exciting prospects of the increased computer utilization brought about by microcomputers is the rapid increase in the quantity and diversity of software design. We have already seen a profound increase in design activity in the "electronic cottage industry" (individuals working at home on their own microcomputers) at nearly all major publishers, and at the many new software houses which have sprung into existence.

There are three aspects of CAI lesson design that must be considered by the CAI author in choosing a CAI lesson design. The first is **function**. What is the instructional or educational function the lesson must serve? Is it to supplement and reinforce an ongoing class? Is it to be the primary means by which the material will be presented? These are the kinds of questions which must be considered when determining the **functional design** of the lesson.

A second aspect of CAI lesson design which must be considered is the **physical** nature of lesson design from the standpoint of computer usage. Some of the constraints on the physical design of the lesson are imposed by the computer to be used, and some are determined by pedagogical considerations. Environmental factors must also be considered when decisions are made about the **physical design** of the lesson.

Finally, the **logical design** of the lesson must be considered. This determination depends largely upon instructional considerations and data such as that which comes out of the learning task analysis performed as a part of the front-end analysis.

FUNCTIONAL DESIGNS

One important way of looking at CAI lesson design is in terms of the instructional function the lesson serves. For example, does it introduce new material, perhaps serving as the primary medium for delivery of instruction, or does it serve mainly to reinforce learning which has occurred by other means?

Drill-and-Practice Design

One of the earliest designs of CAI lessons is the "drill-and-practice" design. It is used to facilitate the learning of material which requires additional reinforcement beyond that which is available within most classroom environments. The drill-and-practice design is most frequently used with material such as spelling or elementary arithmetic.

Typically, drill-and-practice designs involve the semirandom presentation of situations which require fairly simple but precise actions on the part of the student. In some ways, the drill-and-practice design resembles the traditional "flashcard" technique.

Tutorial Design

In the tutorial design, the computer simulates the actions of a very good tutor. In the best of tutorial designs, the computer individualizes the material for the student and keeps accurate records of student progress.

The tutorial design works best for the initial presentation of new material. It also works best with highly verbal material which lends itself to narrative description and question-and-answer techniques.

Gamelike Designs

If the objectives of a CAI lesson can be accomplished with a gamelike approach, the motivation of the students can sometimes benefit greatly. Games are often good for keeping up a rapid pace of learning and increasing the student's affective involvement in the lesson, thereby possibly increasing learning and retention.

Problem-solving Designs

In problem-solving designs, the student uses the microcomputer to actually solve problems. In some problem-solving models the computer is activated to be useful as an "intelligent" calculator which presents problems to the student and then carefully monitors the students actions, step-by-step, as the student attempts the solution. The **process** which the student uses is analyzed at each step and the student is given feedback immediately. In other models, the student only proposes a solution method and the microcomputer carries out the steps. For more complex technical materials such as math or science content, the problem-solving designs allow more realistic learning to take place.

Combined Functional Design

There are some interesting examples of combinations of the functional designs described here into a single synergistic system. In one case that I am aware of arithmetic through the seventh grade is covered by parallel sets of materials in each of these functional designs. The core of the system is a complete tutorial track, which is reinforced by drill-and-practice and timed problem sets. In this case, the timed problem sets are based on the mastery learning concept and the students are expected to produce x answer digits per minute. As a reward, students are allowed to spend time with the game track in which they they enjoy the fruits of their expertise and develop it further. The gamelike designs in this system are particularly imaginative, clever, and motivational.

PHYSICAL DESIGNS

One way of considering the various types of CAI lesson designs is in terms of their simple physical characteristics — primarily in terms of the path the student follows through the lesson. This dimension of CAI lesson design is perhaps the most interesting because it reflects the characteristics and the potential of computer technology. Since such technology is rapidly changing, this aspect of design should be even more intriguing as we witness the continued development of this exciting technology.

Linear Designs

The linear CAI design is the most common of all CAI designs and is likely to remain a popular design for some time to come. It is directly patterned after linear, paper-and-pencil programmed instruction and after a great deal of the CAI courseware which has been written for large computers. Linear CAI fails to exploit the powers of the computer fully, but — it works. And, it is the easiest design to use and to revise or validate. Therefore, it is a good design for the beginning CAI author to use.

In a CAI lesson which has a linear design, each student is presented with the same material as every other student — that is, each student takes exactly the same route through the lesson.

There is sometimes confusion on this issue having to do with the difference between branching as it applies to computer programming and branching as it applies to the instructional logic of a CAI lesson. For example, to a computer programmer, providing different feedback to a student who gives a correct response than is provided to a student who gives an incorrect response is branching. In an instructional sense, and to an instructional designer, it is not.

Spiral Designs

A spiral design draws its name from the fact that the lesson logic flows in a spiral through the material to be learned, each time dwelling on a different property of the material for example. For example, in biology, the spiral design might involve starting with a process such as respiration and seeing how each type of organism, from plants to animals, accomplishes it. The lesson logic might then cover the process of reproduction across all the same organisms.

Branching Designs

A branching lesson is based on an instructional design which includes alternative tracks through the lesson. Depending upon the performance of the student, he or she may see different material than any other student going through the same lesson.

Typically, the branching occurs following a criterion question frame. Students making a correct response would all take the same successive track. Students making incorrect responses would take one or another alternative track, depending upon the exact nature of their incorrect response.

The beauty of branching designs is that they take advantage of the great power of the computer to individualize the lesson and to provide a personalized learning experience for each student. As a result, the student who is capable of moving quickly through a lesson is enabled to do so. The student who needs more time and more practice may also be accomplished.

Later in this chapter we will examine some specific variations of the branching design.

Multitrack Designs

Multitrack — or multilevel — lesson designs as they are also called have material which is written on several distinctly different levels in order to permit the individualization of the lesson.

The top track or highest level is likely to be the shortest. The material is likely to be written more abstractly, at a higher reading level, with less explanation, fewer examples, fewer mnemonics, and with fewer but more difficult questions.

The lowest track is likely to be written with more thorough explanations, more prompting and the like, and is therefore apt to be much longer. If there are additional tracks or levels, they will, of course, be at the appropriate levels in between.

Lesson logic for the multitrack design will typically include a strategy for branching students to another level or leaving them in the same level, depending upon performance.

Regenerative Designs

Regenerative designs are those in which the lesson can generate a different set of problems for each student or for each iteration for the same student. In this way the program seems like a new program each time, since the student sees new examples. The advantage of this is that the student can use the same lesson over and over to strengthen skills.

Some of the newer regenerative lesson designs permit the teacher to specify the type of arithmetic problems the student will see. Still other lesson designs permit the teacher to enter a list of spelling words which the lesson will then present for drill and practice.

Adaptive Designs

Adaptive designs are still quite uncommon, but should be seen more often as time goes on. Adaptive lessons use the data that is accumulated as they are used, with a particular population as a basis for the self-improvement of the lesson. In effect, they "learn" from experience, in somewhat the same way that chess-playing programs get better the more times they play.

LOGICAL DESIGNS

Another way of considering the types of lesson designs is in terms of the logic that governs them. Some lesson designs relate directly to the constructs of formal logic. However, the terminology used to describe lesson logic comes largely from the behavioral psychology of learning. Indeed, CAI lesson design owes much to the development of behavioral learning theory. We should see considerable interesting development in this area as well as in some of the newer lines of investigation, particularly in cognitive psychology as the field matures and the relationship to the work in behavioral psychology gets worked out.

Didactic Designs

The didactic design refers to a lesson design in which the student is presented with information and then asked to respond to questions, basically giving the the same information back. Typically, the student is presented the information in small "steps" and is asked to do minimal synthesis or manipulation of the material. The purpose is more to convey information to the student, to provide him or her with minimum opportunity for practice, and then to check retention, if not understanding.

The didactic lesson design may seem too simple perhaps, but the fact is, it is appropriate for a lot of content.

Discovery Designs

Discovery designs, and the discovery method of learning these designs represent, have attracted a considerable following of devotees who probably go too far in their claims for the universal usefulness of the discovery method. Don't let this distract you from the fact that the discovery design can be very effective when it is used with material for which it is well suited.

Basically, the discovery method involves creating the conditions within which students can reach insights on their own. Normally, students are supplied with only as much material as is needed to reach an insight — about the relationship among a set of facts, for example.

EGRUL Designs

EGRUL is an acronym for a lesson design in which the instructional logic proceeds from example (EG) to rule (RUL). Typically, the student would be provided with training and the opportunity to practice using sets of examples to determine some property which all the members of the class had in common.

As you can see, EGRUL designs are in effect a form of discovery learning. EGRUL and discovery designs both are inductive in nature.

RULEG Designs

RULEG is an acronym for a lesson design in which the instructional logic proceeds from rule (RUL) to example (EG). It is essentially a deductive process.

In a lesson which employs the RULEG design, the student is typically taught to apply a law, principle, or other form of rule to a set of exemplars.

Fading Designs

The term **fading** refers to the fading of prompts. The basic idea is to start with frames containing very strong prompts (as described in chapter 6) and then to change to frames with gradually weaker prompts as the lesson progresses.

The fading design is particularly useful for content which has to be memorized, such as poetry, or anatomy terms.

SOME GENERAL CHARACTERISTICS OF CAI LESSON DESIGNS

The lesson designs described here are meant to serve as examples only. It should be pointed out that nearly all lessons consist of a combination of these designs. It should also be noted that this set of lesson designs is not exhaustive of all the lesson designs that have been or will be used.

The main hope of this author is that you will learn to use these lesson designs in a variety of ways and that you will go on to originate and learn to use other designs. The intention here is to get you started, to expand your repertoire of lesson designs, and to increase your awareness of their existence.

MATCHING CAI LESSON DESIGNS TO LESSON CONTENT

The first consideration in matching lesson design and lesson content is that of function — how the lesson will be used. Will it be used to present original material, or will it be used to reinforce the learning that has taken place in another mode? If it will be used to present new material, it most likely will require a tutorial approach. If it will be used to reinforce learning, a drill-and-practice approach may be called for.

If the content is material that is simple to learn but difficult to remember or apply, or if it is material for which speed of application is an important objective, then the drill-and-practice or perhaps a gamelike design should be chosen.

The condideration of the functional design of the CAI lesson is as much a function of the environmental conditions under which the lesson will be used as it is a pedagogical decision. The characteristics of the learners and what they have the time, interest, and capacity to handle are a major determinate of the functional design of the lesson.

The second consideration which must be made is that of the physical nature of the program. This includes such things as sequence, whether or not additional, adjunctive media will be used, and so forth. Again, the nature of the learners have a lot to do with the decision. Are they likely to have good keyboarding skills? Can they even write? Is there great variability in student skills? Such considerations as these must be made in selecting a physical design for the CAI lesson.

The third kind of decision is far more sophisticated and subtle. It involves not just one decision, but repeated decisions throughout the process of lesson development. I am referring here to the logical design of the lesson. Many different kinds of logical designs may be used in the same lesson, a different one for each lesson segment perhaps.

8

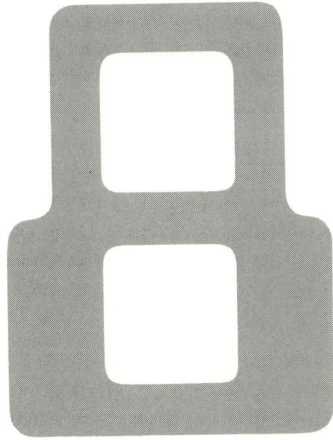

VALIDATION OF CAI LESSONS

To the purist, programmed instruction cannot be considered programmed instruction until it has been validated. To validate a program means to prove its validity empirically, by field-testing it with a sample of students who are representative of the students who will be using the program. It also means doing the revisions indicated and repeating the process of validation until the program meets an acceptable criterion of performance. The criterion might mean that 90 percent of the students must accomplish 90 percent of the objectives. A 90/90 criterion is fairly common, but the criteria must be matched to the students, the material and the conditions under which the lesson will be used.

While high ideals are often expressed for the validation process, the fact remains that few programs have ever been conscientiously validated. In practice, most PI development projects take more time than originally anticipated, and typically the writing itself is finished in a flurry of late-night marathon sessions as the deadline approaches (and just as likely goes by). The result is that there is often no time or money left for the validation process.

CAI lessons should be validated as well, and in much the same way. However, there is currently such a strong demand for CAI courseware that few producers are likely to take the time to validate their products. I have been told that some microcomputer software producers actually run national ads before the software is written and do not even start the writing until sufficient orders are on hand. I don't know if this is true, but I do know that much of the software that has been sold is filled with spelling and grammatical errors which one would assume would be detected and corrected as part of even the most rudimentary validation process.

In the middle of such a seller's market as we are experiencing in the microcomputer CAI courseware field, it is hard to be optimistic that we will see much serious validation of these products very soon. However, this situation will probably change first in those areas which have the potential for a great volume of sales, such as basic skills. Such changes will occur mainly as a result of competition among CAI courseware producers.

I think the large publishing houses will have the effect of raising the quality of CAI courseware, since they have the resources to do so and need to protect their reputations.

Another force which will work for the improvement of standards and for more conscientious validation is a better-informed consumer. As teacher education programs and in-service training in educational applications of computers become more widespread, there will be an increased awareness of what should be expected and demanded of CAI courseware producers.

THE INVALUABLE CRITERION FRAME

The key to effective validation of CAI courseware is the criterion frame. If a criterion frame is written correctly, it will provide good evidence of whether or not the lesson segment that immediately precedes it, in fact, teaches. If the criterion frame is too easy, it can hide the fact that a lesson segment is ineffective.

A well-designed lesson in which the criterion items are appropriately written and well located in the context of the lesson, should not require a posttest. However some people, particularly it seems people with a math or science background, may be more comfortable if all the criterion frames are gathered together and repeated in one place at the end of the lesson and called a posttest. There is no reason that it can't be done this way.

A pretest, however, is another matter. It serves the purpose of checking entry-level knowledge and skills, and allowing you to determine if the students acquired them in your lesson or already had the knowledge and skills upon entering. In this way you can avoid wasting students' time with material they have already mastered.

RECORD KEEPING

One of the most severely debilitating characteristcs of most microcomputer CAI at this point is the rather limited ability to keep a record of student performance. Most systems can only keep track of the number of right and wrong answers, and perhaps compute a percentage ratio. This is inadequate for validation purposes. To properly validate a lesson, the author must know exactly which frames were missed, and exactly what the incorrect answers were. It is also helpful to know how much time the student required to produce each answer — both right and wrong answers. A quick wrong answer can mean that the student is merely careless, or it can mean that he or she is strongly confused. A slow correct answer can mean that the lesson segment preceding it needs some improvement.

Since microcomputer systems used for CAI lack adequate record keeping at this time and are not likely to gain it until their memory capacity is substantially increased, it will be necessary for CAI authors to resort to the same methods which were used by PI authors — namely direct observation of the students as they complete the lessons. Actually the PI author has the edge in this situation by having a written record of what has happened.

Some have advocated that the way around this problem would be to create and validate lessons on a larger system, but make sure that when the lessons were used, they were able to be run on the smaller, less expensive microcomputers likely to be found in the student's environment. I don't know of anyone actually doing this.

EVALUATING STUDENT PERFORMANCE

In many instructional contexts, evaluating student performance is important. It may be for the purpose of assigning a grade, for the purpose of career progression, or, for any one a number of reasons. However, it is important to bear in mind that as far as the validation process is concerned, student performance is only important as an indicator of the effectiveness of the CAI lesson.

EVALUATING LESSON PERFORMANCE

Validation is done solely for the purpose of improving the lesson, and should be seen as an integral part of the developmental process. In fact, the validation process is what makes possible the empirically determined refinement of the CAI lesson.

FIELD TESTING

Whenever possible, field testing should be conducted with members of the same population that the lesson is intended for. One of the tragedies of the PI movement was that programs were used for populations for which they were not originally intended, sometimes with destructive results, which then reflected badly on the technique.

The field testing is best done in stages. The first stage should involve the author or an assistant sitting with one student at a time and carefully observing the student as he or she works through the lesson. In this way, any rough spots that occur in the lesson can be handled directly, and very good notes can be kept on the performance of the lesson.

Following the one-on-one field test, the lesson should be repaired as required. It should then be field-tested with a small group of students simultaneously, to save time. Following the group field test, the lesson is refined further and the process is repeated until the author is satisfied with the lesson.

REVISION

It is the revision process that affords CAI authors the true opportunity to practice and refine their art. The command authors have of the techniques of instructional writing and the extent to which authors can apply these techniques to amplify segments of the lesson which need revision—those factors will determine the power the lesson will eventually have.

The validation will often reveal that a particular lesson segment does not teach. It is up to the CAI author to determine **why** it does not teach, and **what can be done** to make it teach. Sometimes the author can interview the students who had trouble with a specific segment and gain additional insight into the problem.

9

DEVELOPING THE CAI LESSON

THE SYSTEMATIC DEVELOPMENT OF CAI LESSONS

There are two extremes in the CAI courseware development process. At one extreme is the courseware which is developed using all the systematic techniques and procedures that professional instructional systems designers **say** they use. At the other extreme is a mass of courseware that, like Topsy, "just growed." This is the very thing professional instructional designers often accuse others of doing.

Of course, much software is not at either extreme, but rather is found along a continuum. At this time, however, much microcomputer CAI courseware, somewhat in contrast with large-computer CAI courseware, is biased toward the "Topsy" end.

There are several reasons for this. One is simple ignorance. There are just very few people who are familiar with the technology of instructional systems design. A second reason is that even if most of the people now writing CAI courseware for the microcomputer did know what to do, they would still write "quick and dirty" courseware. That's what the competition is doing; there is a press to finish it and get it marketed; it's expensive to spend the time necessary to "do it right"; and the consumers are not sophisticated enough to demand better products — these are some of the reasons for poor quality CAI courseware.

There may indeed be justification for doing this. Many microcomputer users are not able to afford expensive courseware. Unless there is inexpensive CAI courseware available, many users will not be able to afford **any** CAI courseware. This situation gives rise to an interesting philosophical question: Is poor CAI better than no CAI? This question may soon answer itself.

As more microcomputer-oriented CAI courseware is written and used, CAI authors will hopefully become more adept. The competition is certain to become more severe, and users are definitely going to get more sophisticated and demanding. This process is already well underway, and the tempo is certain to increase.

It seems as though another organization or periodical gets into the courseware review-and-evaluation business every week. This means that if you intend to market your CAI courseware, it is certain to come under careful, public scrutiny. The more conscientious a job of development you have done, the better your courseware will fare. Even if you do not plan to market your courseware, you still want it to work.

Documentation is one of the most important parts of any CAI courseware. It is the information that describes the characteristics of the courseware and provides the instructions for its use. Some of the documentation exists on paper, and some of it may be built into the courseware and will appear on the computer screen as the courseware is loaded and as it is run. If your documentation is poor, reviewers will know it; and they may be negative toward your courseware before they ever see it run.

There are other, more immediately compelling benefits to be derived from following systematic courseware development procedures, such as those set out in this chapter.

Developing CAI courseware is a complex task, and it is easy for authors to become hopelessly confused if they are not following a well-structured set of procedures and if their lesson does not have a consistent design. Difficult as it is to keep track of what is going on in the development process, it is nearly impossible to conduct an effective validation if the lesson lacks a coherent design and if vital developmental documents are missing.

WORKING IN TEAMS

One of the best ways around the problem of limited personal knowledge is to work in teams to develop CAI lessons. A team should of course be made up of members whose skills are complementary. If you are deficient in any area of expertise needed for CAI lesson development, don't be afraid to search out someone who can provide that missing skill. It is more productive to be a member of a competent team than it is to stumble along and either never finish a lesson or produce a lesson with a lot of problems.

A QUICK REVIEW

Thus far in the book we have examined the pieces of knowledge and technology which are necessary to the development of a CAI lesson. Now we will examine the process by which they are all fitted together to make a CAI lesson.

We have, for example, seen some of the theoretical underpinnings of CAI. We have examined the ways in which the characteristics of the state-of-the-art microcomputer can be exploited to produce computer assisted instruction. The general technology of the systems approach has been related specifically to the development of CAI lessons.

The special requirements of instructional writing (which in great part CAI really is) have been examined. You have seen a variety of frame protocols which you can model your frames after to enrich your lessons and make them more appropriate. A variety of CAI lesson designs have been discussed. Finally, you have developed a familiarity with the validation process, and hopefully share with me the belief that it is essential.

Now we come to the point at which it all comes together in the form of a CAI lesson.

FRONT-END ANALYSIS

The front-end analysis (FEA) is the most important and often the most neglected and misunderstood part of the development process. FEA is important because if it is done conscientiously, all the succeeding steps of the development process are much easier to carry out, and the lesson is much more likely to be effective.

Determining the subject matter of a CAI lesson is a major part of the front-end analysis (FEA) process.

Choosing Appropriate Content for a CAI Lesson

The professional training — or curriculum — materials developer is typically presented with a problem in human performance. His or her first step is to determine if training is in fact indicated, and if so, which medium is appropriate. Step two (where I would assume most of you are) is setting out to write some CAI, and finding some appropriate content to use.

A very wise person once said, "Any teacher that can be replaced by programmed instruction ought to be." About ten years later, an even wiser person said, "Any program which can be replaced by a teacher, ought to be." The only problem with this reasoning is that it implies that there is no overlap — it implies that material is suitable either for PI or for live instruction. Certainly there is some material that is suitable for both.

The essential truth of the pair of aphorisms, however, is inescapable. The material must be appropriate to the medium.

Generally speaking, the material to be used in a CAI lesson should be material which can be well represented within the symbol set of the microcomputer you have available. For example, it would be hard to create a lesson in statistics on a microcomputer which could not display the special symbols required, such as summation notations and square root symbols.

In order to offset the expenditure of time and resources required to write a CAI lesson, the content chosen should be that which many people need to learn. Material at the elementary school level, in the basic skills, is always a good choice.

The content of a CAI lesson should be material that does not change often. Updating CAI lessons, particularly those written for state-of-the-art microcomputers, is very difficult. Furthermore, you want your lessons to have as long a useful life as possible.

Try to choose material that is simple for you to comprehend, since you will want to put most of your effort into the instructional design process rather than into understanding the content. Try not to choose material which you already have a "pat" way of teaching. In that way you will not be tempted to become too locked into one lesson design. It is important to be able to remain objective so that you are free to choose an appropriate CAI lesson design from among the many alternatives available.

Some individuals seem to develop their CAI courseware as if they believed their courseware was the only curricular material in the discipline area. The fact is, there is a lot of curricular material already in use in the schools which is likely to remain there for a long time. It is not likely that your materials will replace them. The best you can hope for is to have the existing materials "move over a little" and make room for your material.

Since your material will be used along with existing material, you must become familiar with the other material. In that way, you can make your material more useful to teachers who are likely be following the sequence employed in a standard set of curricular materials. Most likely, of course, teachers will be following their own modification of the sequence.

If you break your material into relatively short lesson segments, you will make it easier for teachers to arrange its sequence to match what they are already doing. By so doing, you make your materials more likely to be adopted and used.

For the sake of illustration, I will use a lesson based on five descriptive statistics; mean, median, mode, variance, and standard deviation. I will go through the development of the lesson one step at a time.

Determining the Scope of the Lesson

Particularly for your first lessons, it is wise to select a lesson size which can be accomplished in a reasonable period of time to avoid becoming discouraged. It can take up to two hundred hours to produce a lesson which will take a student approximately one hour to complete. Therefore, select your lesson content with care.

I would suggest that you limit your first attempt at authoring a CAI lesson to a topic which can be accomplished in about twenty criterion frames. Depending upon the subject matter, that should result in a lesson of ten to twenty minutes in length, with probably about sixty to seventy-five frames. Our statistics lesson meets these criteria quite nicely.

Determining Learner Characteristics

It is important to have a fairly specific target population of students in mind. If you are not familiar with the characteristics of the student population you have in mind, you might want to spend some time with a teacher of this grade level. Better yet, you may want to visit a classroom, look at the material which is being used, or even do some substitute teaching at that level if you have the time.

Statistics is typically first taught at the advanced undergraduate level. It is usually assumed that the students have had a first course in algebra, either in high school or early in the college program.

Writing the Rationale

Having collected all the appropriate data and having done all the analytical work required, you are ready to write the rationale. Use this process to clarify your thoughts about the lesson you are going to produce. Discuss your original motive for the undertaking, your expectations for the lesson, and any thing else that will help communicate your intentions.

The written rationale is the first of the process documents associated with the production of your lesson. It is also one which will become part of the permanent documentation to accompany your finished lesson.

The rationale for our sample lesson in statistics is quite simple. The students will learn to calculate certain descriptive statistics, but they will not learn to apply them to a problem, nor will they learn much about the reason for calculating them.

REPRESENTING LESSON CONTENT

It is important for a variety of reasons to represent the expected outcomes of your lesson and its content in a brief, manageable form. This type of process documentation is a necessary working instrument which will facilitate subsequent steps in the lesson creation process. Much of it will also become part of the permanent documentation.

Creating the Topic List

Topic lists are the simplest way of representing the content, or outcomes of the lesson. They are convenient, since they are easily sequenced and resequenced. They also make it easier to determine what should be included and what should be excluded from the lesson. Try to limit topics to one-word descriptors whenever possible. Avoid adjectives or other qualifiers whenever possible. Remember that the topics are just that — topics. They are, in effect, labels which represent more detailed information. The shorter the topics, the easier it is to add them, delete them, and put them in sequence.

The topic list for our sample lesson would look as follows:

1. Mean

2. Median

3. Mode

4. Variance

5. Standard deviation

Creating the Learning Task List

Learning task lists can be created by elaborating the topics of the topic list, although it should not be assumed that there is a one-to-one correspondence. One topic may become several learning task statements or vice versa.

A learning task statement is usually expressed as a brief predicate phrase in the present tense. That is, it usually has a verb in the present tense and an object. For example, a task list might include such items as "Solves equations," "makes ledger entries," or "defines medical terms."

The task list for our sample lesson would be as follows:

1. Calculate the mean of a set of numbers

2. Identify the median of a set of numbers

3. Identify the mode of a set of numbers

4. Calculate the variance of a set of numbers

5. Calculate the standard deviation of a set of numbers

Analyzing Learning Tasks

Learning tasks can be analyzed according to a wide variety of criteria, however for most purposes, only a small subset of criteria are selected which accomplish the author's main purpose.

One of the most commonly used sets of criteria would be one of the learning hierarchies or taxonomies, such as those developed by Robert Gagne[1], Bloom and Krathwohl[2], and other researchers. It is a very worthwhile activity to relate the learning tasks to be covered by your lesson to the levels of such a hierarchy in order to know if you are developing your material at the proper level. It is also important to make certain that your criterion frames and your posttest are of the same level.

For the purposes of our example, I will use four criteria to analyze each learning task on our list. The tasks will be analyzed according to frequency, importance, and difficulty of performance, and category or type of learning. A form such as the one that follows is quite useful for performing the task analysis (fig. 9-1).

[1]Gagne, R. M. The Conditions of Learning, New York: Holt, Rinehart, and Winston, 1965.
[2]Bloom, B. S. et. al., Taxonomy of Educational Objectives, Handbook I: Cognitive Objectives, New York: David McKay Company, Inc., 1975.

```
┌─────────────────────────────────────────────────────────────┐
│                                                               │
│                     TASK ANALYSIS FORM                        │
│                                                               │
└─────────────────────────────────────────────────────────────┘

┌───────────────────────────────────────────────────────────────┐
│ TASK STATEMENT:                                                 │
│                                                                 │
│     Calculate the mean of a set of numbers.                     │
│                                                                 │
└───────────────────────────────────────────────────────────────┘
```

TYPE OF LEARNING	
a. STIMULUS RESPONDING:	
b. MOTOR CHAINING:	
c. VERBAL CHAINING:	
d. MULTIPLE DISCRIMINATION:	
e. CONCEPTS:	
f. PRINCIPLES:	This one.
g. PROBLEM SOLVING:	

OTHER CRITERIA	RATINGS		
	LOW	MEDIUM	HIGH
FREQUENCY			X
IMPORTANCE			X
DIFFICULTY	X		

Fig. 9-1

114

Note that the task statement is simply listed on the form. Then the task statement is classified as to the type of learning involved. In this case it is the application of a principle, or a convention. Problem solving is reserved for tasks which involve the actual creative solution of problems, rather than simple calculations such as this.

This task is also one which is performed quite frequently, and it is important that it be performed correctly because so many statistical calculations include it and so many subsequent steps depend on its accuracy. On the other hand, it is a very simple calculation to perform, involving only the simple arithmetic steps of addition and division.

In figure 9-2 we have a task which only involves the multiple discrimination type of learning, or the identification of something. The task is performed only infrequently, and is of little importance, since few statistical tests build on it. It is also very easy to perform.

```
┌─────────────────────────────────────────────────────────────┐
│                    TASK ANALYSIS FORM                         │
└─────────────────────────────────────────────────────────────┘
```

TASK STATEMENT:

    Identify the median of a set of numbers.

TYPE OF LEARNING
a. STIMULUS RESPONDING:
b. MOTOR CHAINING:
c. VERBAL CHAINING:
d. MULTIPLE DISCRIMINATION: This one.
e. CONCEPTS:
f. PRINCIPLES:
g. PROBLEM SOLVING:

OTHER CRITERIA	RATINGS		
	LOW	MEDIUM	HIGH
FREQUENCY	X		
IMPORTANCE		X	
DIFFICULTY	X		

Fig. 9-2

```
┌─────────────────────────────────────────────────────────┐
│                                                           │
│                  TASK ANALYSIS FORM                       │
│                                                           │
└─────────────────────────────────────────────────────────┘
```

TASK STATEMENT:

    Identify the mode of a set of numbers.

TYPE OF LEARNING
a. STIMULUS RESPONDING:
b. MOTOR CHAINING:
c. VERBAL CHAINING:
d. MULTIPLE DISCRIMINATION: This one.
e. CONCEPTS:
f. PRINCIPLES:
g. PROBLEM SOLVING:

OTHER CRITERIA	RATINGS		
	LOW	MEDIUM	HIGH
FREQUENCY	X		
IMPORTANCE	X		
DIFFICULTY	X		

Fig. 9-3

117

Figure 9-3 involves the same type of learning as the previous task, is used about equally frequently, is even less important, and is also very easy to perform.

```
┌─────────────────────────────────────────────────────────┐
│                                                           │
│                  TASK ANALYSIS FORM                       │
│                                                           │
└─────────────────────────────────────────────────────────┘
```

```
┌─────────────────────────────────────────────────────────┐
│ TASK STATEMENT:                                           │
│                                                           │
│     Calculate the variance of a set of numbers.           │
│                                                           │
└─────────────────────────────────────────────────────────┘
```

```
┌─────────────────────────────────────────────────────────┐
│                   TYPE OF LEARNING                        │
│ --------------------------------------------------------- │
│ a.  STIMULUS RESPONDING:                                  │
│ --------------------------------------------------------- │
│ b.  MOTOR CHAINING:                                       │
│ --------------------------------------------------------- │
│ c.  VERBAL CHAINING:                                      │
│ --------------------------------------------------------- │
│ d.  MULTIPLE DISCRIMINATION:                              │
│ --------------------------------------------------------- │
│ e.  CONCEPTS:                                             │
│ --------------------------------------------------------- │
│ f.  PRINCIPLES:  This one.                                │
│ --------------------------------------------------------- │
│ g.  PROBLEM SOLVING:                                      │
└─────────────────────────────────────────────────────────┘
```

OTHER CRITERIA	RATINGS		
	LOW	MEDIUM	HIGH
FREQUENCY			X
IMPORTANCE			X
DIFFICULTY		X	

Fig. 9-4

Even though calculating the variance (fig. 9-4) is a somewhat more difficult task than calculating the mean (fig. 9-11), for example, it is classified as the same type of learning. It is used very frequently, but is not as important as some of the other tasks, since variance is seldom used by itself, but rather serves as an intermediate step in higher order calculations.

```
┌─────────────────────────────────────────────────────────────┐
│                     TASK ANALYSIS FORM                        │
└─────────────────────────────────────────────────────────────┘
```

TASK STATEMENT:

   Calculate the standard deviation of a set of numbers.

TYPE OF LEARNING

a. STIMULUS RESPONDING:

b. MOTOR CHAINING:

c. VERBAL CHAINING:

d. MULTIPLE DISCRIMINATION:

e. CONCEPTS:

f. PRINCIPLES: This one.

g. PROBLEM SOLVING:

OTHER CRITERIA	RATINGS		
	LOW	MEDIUM	HIGH
FREQUENCY			X
IMPORTANCE			X
DIFFICULTY		X	

Fig. 9-5

121

I have rated this task (fig. 9-5) almost identically with the previous one (fig. 9-4), except that I think it is more important. Feel free to make your own ratings or to ask other people for assistance in making these kinds of ratings.

Writing Objectives

The act of writing the objectives for your lesson will help you to know if you are knowledgeable enough of your subject matter or not. If you have trouble writing them, you may need to do some homework or seek out some other form of assistance.

I advocate the use of a form for writing objectives, such as the one shown in chapter four. Objective forms completed for our five topics appear on the following pages (figs. 9-6. through 9-10).

```
┌─────────────────────────────────────────────────────────────┐
│                 OBJECTIVE DEVELOPMENT FORM                    │
└─────────────────────────────────────────────────────────────┘

┌─────────────────────────────────────────────────────────────┐
│ TOPIC:                                                        │
│          MEAN                                                 │
├─────────────────────────────────────────────────────────────┤
│ CONDITIONS:                                                   │
│                                                               │
│   GIVEN A SET OF NUMBERS SUCH AS SCORES OR OTHER MEASURES...  │
│                                                               │
├─────────────────────────────────────────────────────────────┤
│ BEHAVIOR:                                                     │
│                                                               │
│   ...ADD THE NUMBERS AND DIVIDE BY THEIR FREQUENCY            │
│   TO CALCULATE THEIR MEAN...                                  │
│                                                               │
├─────────────────────────────────────────────────────────────┤
│ CRITERIA:                                                     │
│                                                               │
│   ...WITH 90% ACCURACY, 90% OF THE TIME,                      │
│   AT A RATE OF 40 ANSWER DIGITS PER MINUTE.                   │
│                                                               │
└─────────────────────────────────────────────────────────────┘
```

Fig. 9-6

```
┌─────────────────────────────────────────────────────┐
│              OBJECTIVE DEVELOPMENT FORM               │
└─────────────────────────────────────────────────────┘
```

```
┌───────────────────────────────────────────────────────────┐
│ TOPIC:                                                      │
│          MEDIAN                                             │
├───────────────────────────────────────────────────────────┤
│ CONDITIONS:                                                 │
│                                                             │
│    GIVEN A SET OF NUMBERS REPRESENTING TEST SCORES          │
│    OR OTHER NUMBERS UP TO THREE DIGITS...                   │
├───────────────────────────────────────────────────────────┤
│ BEHAVIOR:                                                   │
│                                                             │
│                                                             │
│    ...EXAMINE THEM TO DETERMINE AND IDENTIFY                │
│    THEIR MEDIAN VALUE...                                    │
│                                                             │
│                                                             │
├───────────────────────────────────────────────────────────┤
│ CRITERIA:                                                   │
│                                                             │
│    ...WITHIN 30 SECONDS, WITH 90% ACCURACY, 90% OF THE TIME.│
│                                                             │
│                                                             │
│                                                             │
└───────────────────────────────────────────────────────────┘
```

Fig. 9-7

```
┌─────────────────────────────────────────────────────┐
│                                                       │
│           OBJECTIVE DEVELOPMENT FORM                  │
│                                                       │
└─────────────────────────────────────────────────────┘

┌─────────────────────────────────────────────────────┐
│  TOPIC:                                               │
│          MODE                                         │
│                                                       │
├─────────────────────────────────────────────────────┤
│  CONDITIONS:                                          │
│                                                       │
│      GIVEN A SET OF NUMBERS SUCH AS TEST SCORES...    │
│                                                       │
│                                                       │
├─────────────────────────────────────────────────────┤
│  BEHAVIOR:                                            │
│                                                       │
│                                                       │
│      ...EXAMINE THE NUMBERS TO DETERMINE THEIR MODAL VALUE... │
│                                                       │
│                                                       │
├─────────────────────────────────────────────────────┤
│  CRITERIA:                                            │
│                                                       │
│      ...WITH 90% ACCURACY, 90% OF THE TIME,          │
│      WITHIN 30 SECONDS.                               │
│                                                       │
│                                                       │
└─────────────────────────────────────────────────────┘
```

Fig. 9-8

```
┌─────────────────────────────────────────────────────────┐
│                                                           │
│              OBJECTIVE DEVELOPMENT FORM                   │
│                                                           │
└─────────────────────────────────────────────────────────┘

┌─────────────────────────────────────────────────────────┐
│  TOPIC:                                                   │
│           VARIANCE                                        │
│                                                           │
├─────────────────────────────────────────────────────────┤
│  CONDITIONS:                                              │
│                                                           │
│     GIVEN A SET OF NUMBERS UP TO THREE DIGITS EACH...     │
│                                                           │
│                                                           │
├─────────────────────────────────────────────────────────┤
│  BEHAVIOR:                                                │
│     ...CALCULATE THE AVERAGE AMOUNT OF VARIANCE FROM      │
│     THE MEAN THAT EXISTS WITHIN THE SET OF NUMBERS...     │
│                                                           │
│                                                           │
│                                                           │
├─────────────────────────────────────────────────────────┤
│  CRITERIA:                                                │
│     ...WITH 90% ACCURACY, 90% OF THE TIME,                │
│     WORKING AT RATE OF 40 ANSWER DIGITS PER MINUTE.       │
│                                                           │
│                                                           │
│                                                           │
└─────────────────────────────────────────────────────────┘
```

Fig 9-9

```
┌─────────────────────────────────────────────────────────────┐
│                  OBJECTIVE DEVELOPMENT FORM                   │
└─────────────────────────────────────────────────────────────┘
```

```
┌─────────────────────────────────────────────────────────────┐
│ TOPIC:                                                        │
│           STANDARD DEVIATION                                  │
│                                                               │
├─────────────────────────────────────────────────────────────┤
│ CONDITIONS:                                                   │
│                                                               │
│     GIVEN A SET OF NUMBERS UP TO THREE DIGITS EACH...         │
│                                                               │
│                                                               │
├─────────────────────────────────────────────────────────────┤
│ BEHAVIOR:                                                     │
│                                                               │
│                                                               │
│     ...CALCULATE THEIR STANDARD DEVIATION FROM THE MEAN...    │
│                                                               │
│                                                               │
│                                                               │
├─────────────────────────────────────────────────────────────┤
│ CRITERIA:                                                     │
│         ...WITH 90% ACCURACY, 90% OF THE TIME,                │
│     AT A RATE OF 40 ANSWER DIGITS PER MINUTE.                 │
│                                                               │
│                                                               │
│                                                               │
└─────────────────────────────────────────────────────────────┘
```

Fig. 9-10

127

Note that the objective forms could have been filled in with much more cryptic entries than I have used here and still be useful. However, having completed them as I have, I can either write them out in continuous sentences, verbatim, or in abbreviated form for convenience.

1. Given a set of numbers such as scores or other measures, add the numbers and divide by their frequency to calculate their mean, with 90% accuracy, 90% of the time, at a rate of 40 answer digits per minute.
2. Given a set of numbers representing test scores or other numbers up to three digits, examine them to determine and identify their median value, within 30 seconds, with 90% accuracy, 90% of the time.
3. Given a set of numbers, such as test scores, examine the numbers to determine their modal value, with 90% accuracy, 90% of the time, within 30 seconds.
4. Given a set of numbers up to three digits each, calculate the average amount of variance from the mean that exists within the set of numbers, with 90% accuracy, 90% of the time, working at a rate of 40 answer digits per minute.
5. Given a set of numbers up to three digits each, calculate their standard deviation from the mean, with 90% accuracy, 90% of the time, at a rate of 40 answer digits per minute.

After you have completed your objectives, show them to others who are knowledgeable of the subject matter area to elicit their feedback and advice. Most people will be happy to read and react to your objectives.

Writing the Criterion Frames

Writing the criterion frames can either be done at this point or deferred until the lesson creation phase. If you choose to do so, you have enough information to write them at this point. The criterion frames often have a one-to-one correspondence to the objectives. You may not be able to sequence the criterion frames at this point, but that can come later.

A **coding form** can be a great help in writing the CAI lesson. It allows the CAI author to lay out the frame formats, sequence and resequence the lesson, and generally to keep track of what is going on in the lesson. It is also very helpful during the validation process, providing a convenient place to record validation data.

I have designed a coding form which you may wish to use as it is or modify to suit the authoring process you are using. I have used it here to carry the statistics example further, by writing a criterion frame for each topic (figs. 9-11 through 9-15).

```
┌─────────────────────────────────────────────────────────────┐
│                  CAI LESSON CODING FORM                       │
└─────────────────────────────────────────────────────────────┘

AUTHOR:_____    DATE:_____

LESSON:_____    SEGMENT:_____

TOPIC:_____    FRAME NUMBER:_____

REVISION NUMBER:_____  VALIDATION DATA:_____
```

LINE #	OP CODE	LESSON CONTENT
		5 10 15 20 25 30 35 40
		· 1
		· 2
		CALCULATE THE MEAN OF THE 3
		FOLLOWING TEST SCORES: 4
		· 5
		SALLY 86 JAMIE 94 6
		BILLY 68 JANE 76 7
		JOHNNY 85 BETTY 65 8
		GREG 72 MARY 82 9
		SHIRLEY 91 PHYLLIS 88 10
		DONNY 85 GARY 79 11
		· 12
		ANSWER:_____ 13
		· 14
		· 15
		· 16

Fig. 9-11

130

CAI LESSON CODING FORM

AUTHOR:_____ DATE:_____

LESSON:_____ SEGMENT:_____

TOPIC:_____ FRAME NUMBER:_____

REVISION NUMBER:_____ VALIDATION DATA:_____

LINE #	OP CODE	LESSON CONTENT								
		5	10	15	20	25	30	35	40	
		. . . .								1
		. . . .								2
		. . . .								3
		. . . .								4
		. . . .								5
		IDENTIFY THE MEDIAN OF THE FOLLOWING								6
		RANGE OF NUMBERS:								7
		. . . .								8
		23, 23, 24, 26, 27, 27, 28, 30, 31, 32								9
		32, 33, 34, 35, 37, 40, 42, 43, 43, 45								10
		. . . .								11
		ANSWER:_____								12
		. . . .								13
		. . . .								14
		. . . .								15
		. . . .								16

Fig. 9-12

```
┌─────────────────────────────────────────────────────────────┐
│                  CAI LESSON CODING FORM                       │
└─────────────────────────────────────────────────────────────┘

┌─────────────────────────────────────────────────────────────┐
│  AUTHOR:_____  DATE:_____    │
│                                                               │
│  LESSON:_____  SEGMENT:_____   │
│                                                               │
│  TOPIC:_____  FRAME NUMBER:_____   │
│                                                               │
│  REVISION NUMBER:_____  VALIDATION DATA:_____    │
└─────────────────────────────────────────────────────────────┘
```

LINE #	OP CODE	LESSON CONTENT	
		5 10 15 20 25 30 35 40	
		....	1
		....	2
		....	3
		....	4
		WHAT IS THE MODE OF THE FOLLOWING	5
		SET OF NUMBERS?	6
			7
		18, 19, 23, 22, 28, 21, 21, 26, 22	8
		23, 25, 26, 20, 27, 22, 20, 19, 25	9
			10
		ANSWER:_____	11
		....	12
		....	13
		....	14
		....	15
		....	16

Fig. 9-13

```
┌─────────────────────────────────────────────────────────────┐
│                  CAI LESSON CODING FORM                       │
└─────────────────────────────────────────────────────────────┘

┌─────────────────────────────────────────────────────────────┐
│ AUTHOR:_____  DATE:_____     │
│                                                               │
│ LESSON:_____  SEGMENT:_____    │
│                                                               │
│ TOPIC:_____  FRAME NUMBER:_____   │
│                                                               │
│ REVISION NUMBER:_____  VALIDATION DATA:_____   │
└─────────────────────────────────────────────────────────────┘
```

LINE #	OP CODE	LESSON CONTENT

```
                 5    10    15    20    25    30    35    40

.................................................................  1
.................................................................  2
.................................................................  3
.................................................................  4
      WHAT IS THE VARIANCE OF THE FOLLOWING
.................................................................  5
      NUMBERS?
.................................................................  6
.................................................................  7
      6, 3, 9, 8, 9, 12, 11, 10, 7, 8, 5, 9
.................................................................  8
      10, 9, 4, 4, 12, 6, 9, 11, 8, 6, 7, 3
.................................................................  9
.................................................................  10
                 THE VARIANCE IS:_____
.................................................................  11
.................................................................  12
.................................................................  13
.................................................................  14
.................................................................  15
.................................................................  16
```

Fig. 9-14

133

CAI LESSON CODING FORM

AUTHOR:_____ DATE:_____

LESSON:_____ SEGMENT:_____

TOPIC:_____ FRAME NUMBER:_____

REVISION NUMBER:_____ VALIDATION DATA:_____

LINE #	OP CODE	LESSON CONTENT	
		5 10 15 20 25 30 35 40	
		....	1
		....	2
		....	3
		....	4
		WHAT IS THE STANDARD DEVIATION OF THE	5
		FOLLOWING SET OF NUMBERS?	6
		....	7
		54, 36, 42, 45, 45, 48, 32, 53, 54, 50	8
		48, 47, 39, 49, 37, 52, 34, 38, 55, 45	9
		....	10
		THE STANDARD DEVIATION IS:_____	11
		....	12
		....	13
		....	14
		....	15
		....	16

Fig. 9-15

DESIGNING THE LESSON

This is perhaps the most critical phase of all. If the design phase is done properly, the rest of the development work can be very easy. If not, many problems can be encountered.

Determining CAI Lesson Design

A good task analysis should yield most of the information that you will need to select the appropriate lesson design or combination of designs.

You will recall from chapter 7 that there are actually three design decisions to be made. The first design decision concerns the functional design of the lesson — that is, drill-and-practice, tutorial, gamelike, and so on. The second design decision involves a consideration of the physical design (in great part, the sequence) of the lesson — that is, linear, branching, spiral, and so on. The third type of design decision is concerned with the logical design of the lesson — didactic, discovery, EGRUL, and so forth.

At the functional level, our sample lesson will involve both a tutorial and drill-and-practice design — we must present information on the descriptive statistics involved, and then provide practice applying the principles to sets of numbers. The physical design of the sample lesson is linear, with only limited branching of the recursive type. The logical design of the lesson is RULEG.

Developing the Systems Flow Chart

Recall from chapter 4 that the systems flow chart is used to represent the major parts of the CAI lesson, usually the criterion frames, and to arrange them in the sequence that the lesson will follow. Recall further that the systems flow chart is usually made up of only three types of symbols — the terminator symbol, the operations box, and the decision box.

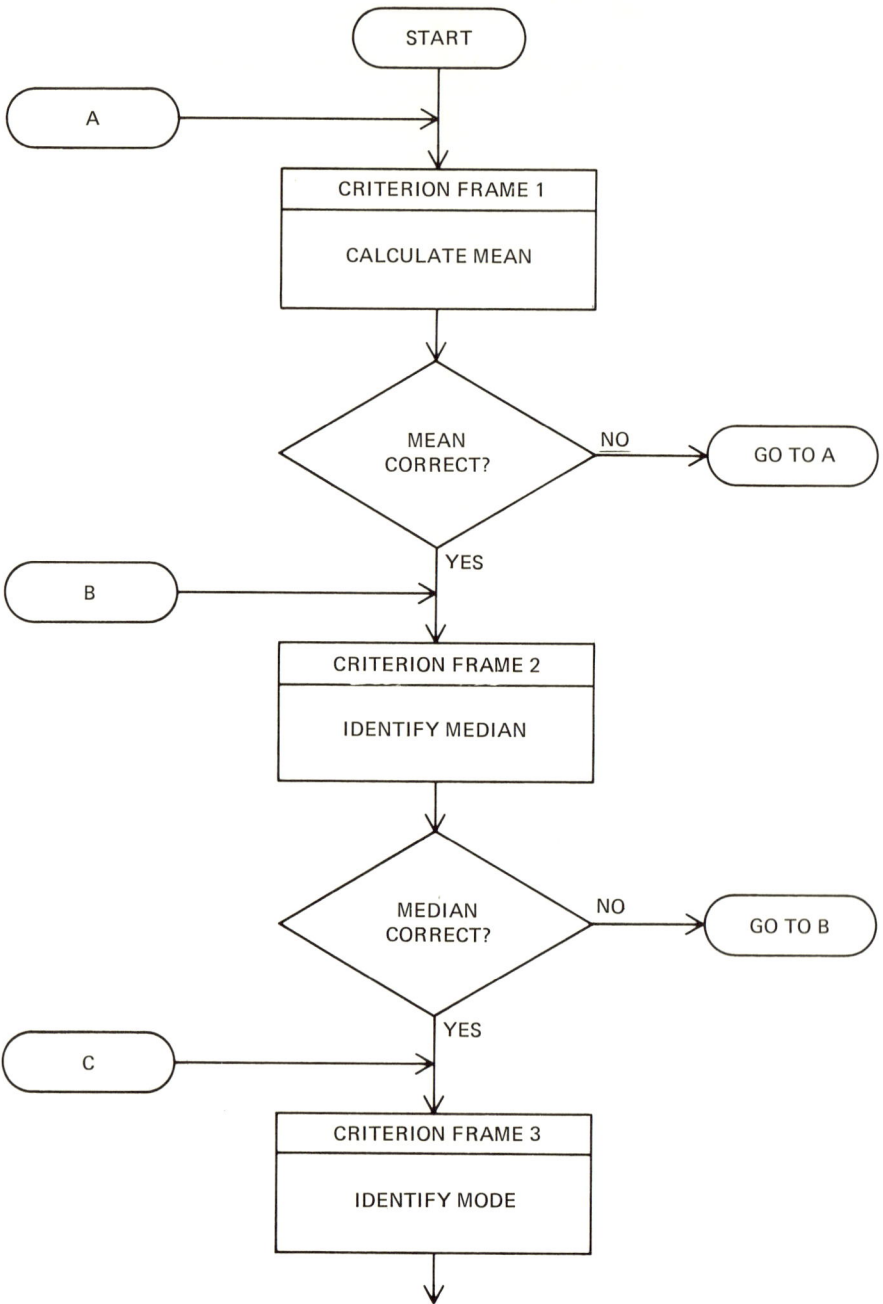

Fig. 9-16

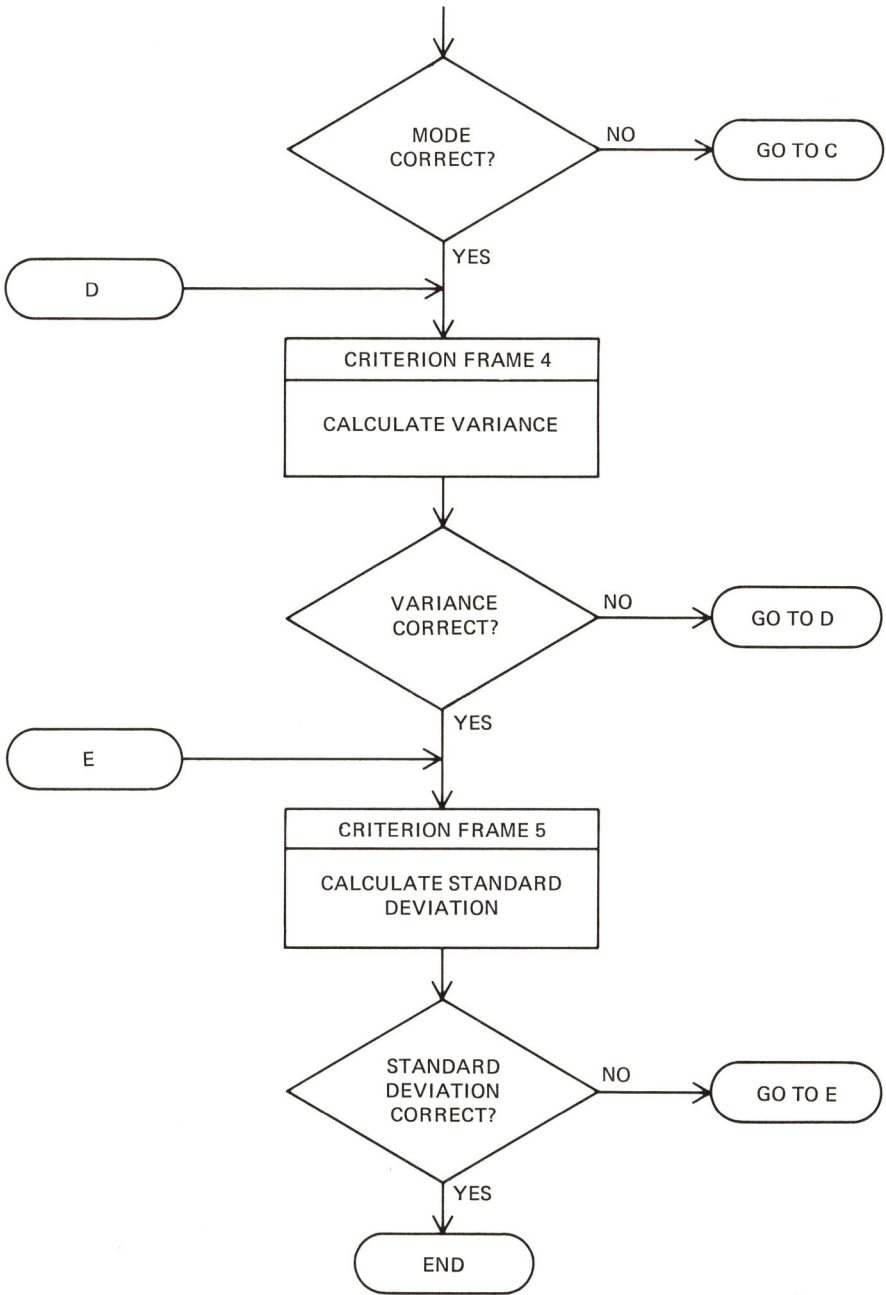

Fig. 9-16 (continued)

In figure 9-16   there is a one-to-one relationship between the flow chart elements and the criterion frames. Each operations box represents a criterion frame, and each decision box represents the outcome of the student's performance on the preceding criterion frame.

Developing the Detailed Flow Chart

For purposes of illustration, we will only show a portion of a detailed flow chart created by adding detail to the systems flow chart. A detailed flow chart can be made to show everything, right down to the way in which each response is judged and all the alternative branches that are taken. However, such detail is usually unnecessary.

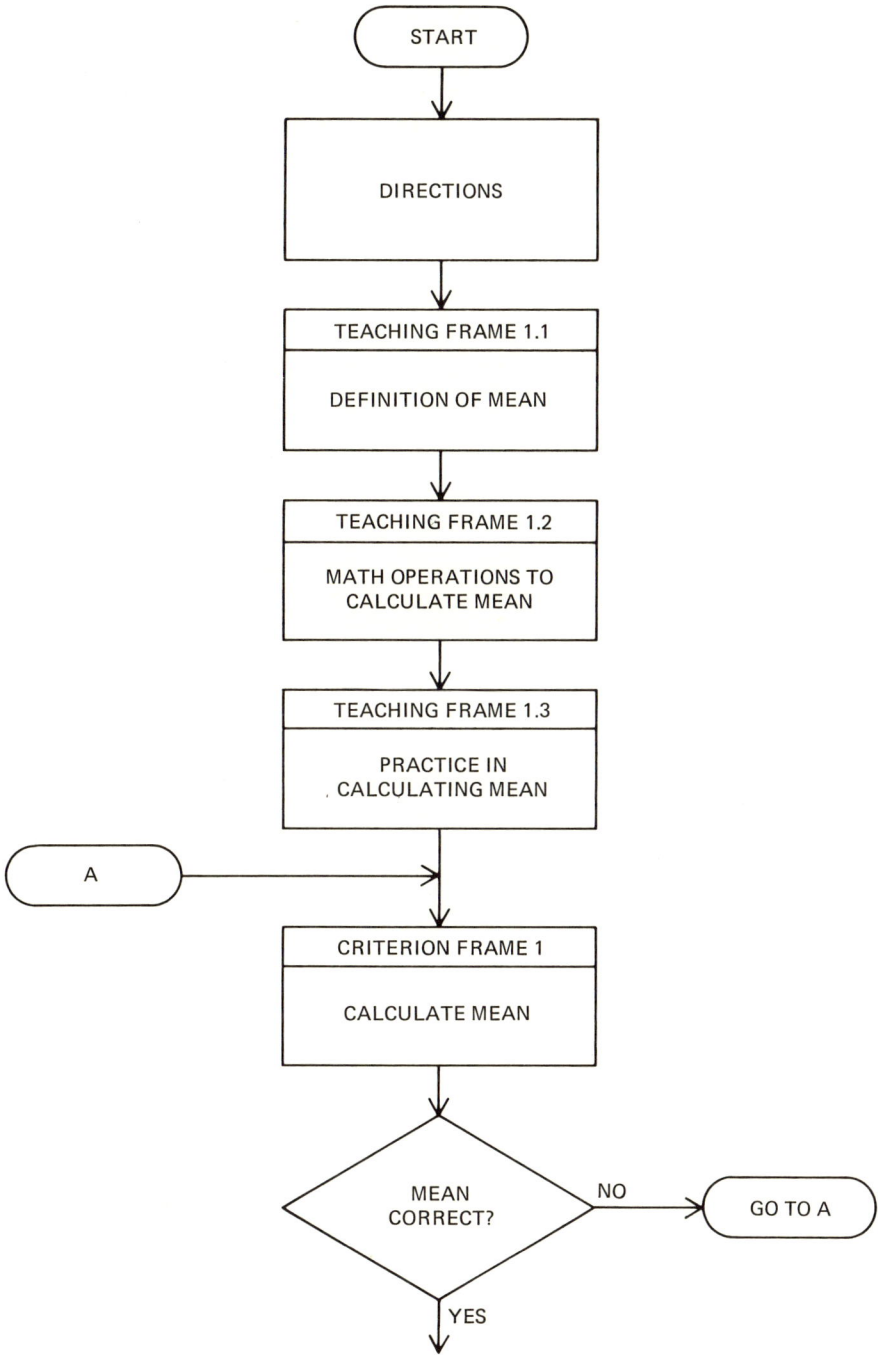

Fig. 9-17

Here (fig. 9-17) we will basically add directions and teaching frames to create the detailed flow chart. The remainder of the detailed flow chart would be constructed in the same way as this segment was. Feel free to originate techniques for flowcharting that suit your style.

CREATING THE LESSON

Now we are finally ready to begin the actual construction of the lesson itself. We have done the front-end analysis, represented the content in various symbolic ways, selected a lesson design, and flowcharted the lesson.

Selecting a Production Strategy

The strategy you will use in the actual development of the lesson will be determined by several factors in addition to your own preferences. One of the main factors is author language, or the authoring system you will use. This, of course, will be determined by your skill level (or the assistance you have available), the software those who will use the lesson have available, and the time you can allow for creating the lesson. A second factor is the amount of resources you have available, including time, money, and test subjects for validation cycles. The material which follows suggests three possible production strategies and some of the reasons for adopting each.

Strategy I

Strategy I is used when you have a tremendous amount of time, test subjects and perhaps money for the validation process. Given these conditions, you can afford as many validation cycles as it takes to create a well-functioning lesson by successively improving it.

Under strategy I, the author would create a lesson which consisted exclusively of criterion frames and then administer it to a set of students. The author would then examine the effectiveness of the lesson. Very likely, some of the teaching frames would do their job consistently. For those criterion frames, it would not be necessary to write any teaching frames.

The author would then create only the most minimal set of teaching frames necessary to back up those criterion frames which did not work in the previous validation cycle. The lesson would then be passed through another validation cycle, revised, and so on, until it worked with as high a degree of reliability as required.

If our sample lesson was to be developed under stategy I, we would need only to use the criterion frames written in this example, to write the code to drive them, and to enter them into the computer.

Strategy II

Strategy II is a more realistic approach. In strategy II, a lesson is written which is intended to be a complete program, but is very "lean." The author knows that teaching frames will have to be added and strengthened. However, frames are only added on the basis of validation data. This is the strategy to be used most of the time, since it is a sensible compromise which results in an efficient lesson with a minimum of cost in time, money, and effort.

The lesson component represented by the segment of detailed flow chart (fig. 9-17) would be appropriate for strategy II. In it we anticipated only one teaching frame for each aspect to be taught. Most likely if the lesson were put through a validation cycle in this form, it would turn out that additional teaching frames were required.

Strategy III

Strategy III represents a situation which is encountered all too often. The author writes a lesson which must be considered to be complete as written (often due to conditions beyond his or her control). The author knows he or she will not have time or opportunity to rewrite the lesson or improve it on the basis of empirical validation data, since it will not be validated. Unfortunately, most of the CAI courseware which is currently being written for microcomputers is written using strategy III.

Writing the Script

On most microcomputers at the present state of the art, you will no doubt find it easier to write out a script for your lessons prior to keying them into the computer. In fact, many people find it useful to use specially prepared coding forms such as the one I included earlier in this chapter. Such a form allows the CAI author to lay out the frames exactly as they will appear on the screen. Note that there are columns provided for the coding which must be provided if you are using a computer language rather than a CAI authoring system. In the case of our example, it will be assumed that the PILOT CAI author language is being used.

Think of the coding forms as comprising a script which you are writing for the microcomputer to follow. The coding forms should be retained, even after the lesson has been entered into the microcomputer. You will find the script to be invaluable in the validation and revision process.

Writing the Criterion Frames

If the criterion frames were not written as part of the design stage, they must be written at this point. Recall that in chapter 6 the construction of criterion frames was discussed. Some of the possible forms that criterion frames can take were also discussed.

The exact form each of the criterion frames will take is primarily a result of consideration of the task analysis. In this way, the format of the frame is related to the expected learning outcomes. If the outcome expectation is that students merely "recognize" a set of terms, for example, it is unwise to ask them to "generate" or "recall" the terms.

A second factor to be considered is the learner population and the competence they are likely to have. If your students are young children, you will have to adjust the reading level of your frames accordingly, and not ask them to write words they should not be responsible for learning how to spell.

Writing the Teaching Frames

The teaching frames are nearly always written directly in support of the succeeding criterion frame. Chapter 6 provided you with a variety of frame protocols which you can draw upon in creating your teaching frames. Try to match the teaching frames to the criterion frame which follows as regards the level of learning, the reading level, and so forth.

Teaching frames need not always take the form of a question. They can also be in simple narrative form. However, try to avoid the pattern in which narrative frames simply alternate with question frames. That approach is very boring for the student and is a weak instructional approach.

Writing the Directions

After the instructional design has been determined and the frames have been written (thus determining the frame formats), it is relatively easy to write the directions. Certainly, some of the directions will have been written as the frames were written. However, you will find that it is easier to plan the directions at the later stage and to put them in at exactly the right place, thereby avoiding unnecessary redundancy.

Developing a Record-Keeping Strategy

Unless you are using a CAI authoring system in which it is automatically taken care of, you will need to design a record-keeping system for your lesson. This is a good time to do that, since it will likely affect your other coding but cannot be done until you know rather precisely what the lesson will look like.

Coding the Lesson

Once the script is complete, containing criterion frames, teaching frames, and directions, it is possible to code the computer instructions. Depending on the language or the authoring system you will be using, you will proceed differently at this point. If you are using an authoring system, you can proceed to enter the script according to the menu instructions and options.

If you are using a language, you will most likely want to write out the code, or the instructions to the computer, on paper first, and then enter everything into the computer at once. Most coding forms for CAI lessons provide columns for the coding and line numbers, as well as for the lesson content.

AUTHOR:_____ DATE:_____

LESSON:_____ SEGMENT:_____

TOPIC:_____ FRAME NUMBER:_____

REVISION NUMBER:_____ VALIDATION DATA:_____

LINE #	OP CODE	LESSON CONTENT	
		5 10 15 20 25 30 35 40	
*LAB	T:		
	T:	....	1
	T:	....	2
	T.	CALCULATE THE MEAN OF THE	
	T:	FOLLOWING TEST SCORES.	3
	T:		4
	T:	SALLY 86 JAMIE 94	5
	T:	BILLY 68 JANE 76	6
	T:	JOHNNY 85 BETTY 65	7
	T:	GREG 72 MARY 82	8
	T:	SHIRLEY 91 PHYLLIS 88	9
	T:	DONNY 85 GARY 79	10
	T:		11
	T:		12
	T:	ANSWER:_____	13
	T:		14
	T:		15
	T.		16

Fig. 9-18

144

For illustration purposes, one frame of the sample lesson will be coded here using the PILOT CAI authoring language (see fig. 9-18). Note that we have included a label in the first column and that only a single operations code (op code) of **T:** is required for each line of the screen.

We must provide for some other things at this point. We must give the microcomputer the anticipated correct answer(s) with which to compare the students' answers, as well as an indication of the anticipated incorrect answer(s). We must also tell the computer what we want it to say to the student in each case, and then, where we want it to branch to next.

Creating Graphics

If graphics are to be included, they should be designed and layed out on paper at this point. On many systems the graphics must be created in a different mode or even in a different language than that used to code the CAI itself.

Debugging the Coding

After the entire program has been entered into the microcomputer, it must be test run. Unless you have incredible luck, it will have bugs and require considerable revision, technically referred to as **debugging.** The debugging often takes more time than the original coding itself, so don't get discouraged, but be sure you leave enough time for it. One of the most frequent complaints about courseware is that it has been distributed with bugs in it.

Writing Adjunctive Material

If your lesson will include adjunct material, this is the time to create it or to finalize it. Ideally, it should be created in such a way that it directly supports one or more criterion frames. In this way its effectiveness can be determined just as if it were part of the lesson proper.

VALIDATING THE LESSON

The thing to keep in mind during the validation process is that you are testing the CAI lesson, **not** the students. Therefore, the testing process is considerably different from a traditional classroom testing situation. One of the main differences is in the distribution of test items. In the validation process, the test items must be comprehensive, with at least one item related to each testable segment of the lesson. In a traditional classroom testing situation, it is customary to use a representative sample of test items.

The items are also designed to test slightly different things. For example, the items should be matched to the instructional intent of the lesson as indicated by the learning task analysis, rather than going beyond it.

Developing a Frame Identification Strategy

In order to perform a meaningful validation, there must be a way to relate validation data to the frames they refer to. One of the best ways to do this is to index the frames on the script and on either the detailed flow chart or the systems flow chart. Most systems unfortunately do not permit you to include frame identifiers on a temporary basis and then remove them after the validation is completed. Perhaps someday they will and the validation process will, be made easier.

Writing the Pretest

The pretest serves two purposes. One is to determine that students have the necessary prerequisites for the lesson, and the other is to determine that the students don't already have the knowledge and skills that the lesson is designed to develop. As mentioned above, the pretest must be comprehensive, as it is the base line against which accomplishment on the posttest will be measured. It is the difference between the pretest data and the posttest data that indicates the success of the CAI lesson.

Writing the Posttest

The posttest can be almost identical to the pretest except that it should not test for entering skills. It also should not be exactly identical; otherwise the student will exhibit improvement based simply on practice effects from taking the two tests.

Conducting the Field Test

The first stage of the field test should usually involve you sitting and observing the first one or two students going through the material. In that way you can holistically observe any difficulties that the student may encounter, and help the student past them on a one-to-one basis. Armed with this firsthand knowledge you will almost certainly have to make repairs to all aspects of the lesson, from coding to text to directions.

Following the one-on-one testing and the revision it indicates needs to be done, you will most likely be confident that the lesson will function reasonably well on its own. You will then want to test the materials with a small group of students all at the same time.

The number of validation cycles will be a function of the number of repairs your lesson needs after each cycle and the amount of time you have available.

Now It Becomes a CAI Lesson

Only after you have put your lesson through a number of validation cycles and it is working well should you consider it to be a CAI lesson. It is really the validation process and your creative use of the kinds of amplification techniques discussed earlier that gives the CAI lesson that special magic of teaching power and efficiency.

DOCUMENTATION

The term used to refer to the descriptive material which accompanies the program and explains its purpose and use is **documentation.** Generally speaking, and all other things being equal, software or programs which are accompanied by good, complete, easy-to-use documentation will be much more accepted than others.

Documentation may be either written paper documents or remarks which are included in the software itself and appear on the screen. Good built-in documentation is an immense help, but almost never eliminates the need for paper documentation.

A specialized form of documentation are the **diagnostics** which appear on the screen when the operator makes an error, or when there is a software or system fault. Typically, diagnostic statements are brief, and are more fully explained in the paper documentation.

In the case of CAI lessons, there is a special burden placed on the author for documentation. In addition to the usual norms of documentation in the computer field, the CAI author must satisfy the need for validation data and such other information as may be necessary to facilitate adoption decisions.

Good documentation should contain several vital pieces of information. For example, it should clearly describe the environment in which the lesson must run, that is, microcomputer model, disk or tape, memory size, special hardware modifications, software, and so forth.

All the necessary run instructions should be clearly provided. Aim your run instructions as well as all other documentation at the least knowledgeable user. Keep your language simple, clear, and complete. Above all, test your instructions by having someone who is minimally knowledgeable with computers try to follow them.

One of the most important things you can provide for a teacher considering the adoption of your CAI lesson is the average amount of time students are likely to require to complete the material. It would also be helpful to indicate the degree to which teacher assistance is required by the lesson.

Many of the process documents used in the developmental process should be included either as is or in a modified form in the documentation — for example, the rationale, the objectives, the task analysis, and the validation data. The validation data should, of course, be in reduced form — for example, 40 third grade students at such and such elementary school served as the validation population. Ninety percent of them accomplished ninety percent of the objectives.

10

CAI
COURSEWARE
REVIEW

WHY IS CAI COURSEWARE REVIEWED?

Courseware reviewers, whose work appears in microcomputer magazines, journals, and other organs in ever increasing frequency, are probably attempting to fill two needs. One is to simply focus attention on the CAI courseware that is available, to provide an information service for teachers and others who are searching for CAI courseware. A second, and usually secondary, motive is to evaluate the courseware and tell the potential user things about the courseware that the supplier may fail to mention.

Such reviews are steadily becoming more critical as the sophistication of the field increases. This is a good trend. There is evidence that negative reviews have already resulted in the improvement of courseware which had already been released. As more and more courseware is created, the competition for sales will increase, and the reviews will have an even greater effect.

What this means for the CAI author is that it is not too soon to begin observing high standards of authorship, since nearly all courseware is likely to be reviewed in the public media, and such reviews will have a great deal to do with the success of the courseware in the marketplace.

ANTICIPATE REVIEW

You should always anticipate that your CAI courseware is going to be reviewed. There are some things that you can do to improve your chances of getting a good review, in addition to creating good lessons, of course. In this chapter I will discuss some of the main parameters that reviewers cover so that you can become familiar with them. Probably no single reviewer covers all these points. Indeed, some of the aspects discussed here I have never seen covered in a review, but I expect they will be covered eventually.

Some of the characteristics included reflect concerns I have heard teachers express about CAI courseware they were considering adopting. Don't forget, teachers will probably make most of the adoption decisions and will be responsible for making the courseware work in the classroom.

AUTHOR-SUPPLIED INFORMATION

One way to insure that your courseware gets good reviews is to put out good, complete, accurate information about it. In this way, you can make sure that none of its virtues gets overlooked.

Documentation

You have to supply documentation with your courseware anyway, so why not make sure that it is as complete as possible and fully describes the strengths of your lessons. Make sure that if you have conscientiously validated your courseware, all the detailed validation data is included in your documentation. This fact will set your courseware "a cut above" for quite some time to come.

Sales Support Materials

Take advantage of sales support materials, such as brochures and press releases, to blow your own horn and tell the strengths of your courseware over again.

REVIEWER'S CONTRIBUTIONS

Reviewers have already made significant contributions to the improvement of courseware. Although it can be unpleasant to get a negative review, you should look upon it as a service which will encourage you to improve your courseware.

The other side of the coin is the prospect that a good review will give your courseware publicity and stimulate demand for it.

CATEGORIES OF INFORMATION ABOUT CAI COURSEWARE

The sections that follow are a composite of things that do, or should, show up in courseware reviews. By becoming familiar with them, you can be in a better position to receive reviews. They can also serve as a guide if you are in a position to select courseware or are asked to write a review of someone else's courseware.

USER INFORMATION

This category of information is largely descriptive information that teachers or other people in a position to use courseware need to know. It also includes the information needed to manage the CAI lesson in an environment with students.

Source

The prospective user would have to know where he or she can get the courseware. A lot of courseware is available from a single source, usually its author. It

is not necessarily a bad idea for authors to distribute
their own wares, but the prospective user should be aware
of this so as not to waste a lot of time looking for the
courseware in stores.

Availability

Some courseware, such as that written under
government grants, can be very difficult to obtain. I
had the frustrating experience of trying to obtain copies
of films that were developed under a government grant,
but the rights had been sold to a publisher, and the
publisher was not sure whether it wanted to sell copies
or what to charge for them.

Documentation

Documentation is an important part of the courseware
package. Unfortunately, there is a wide divergence of
opinion as to what constitutes adequate documentation.
There seems to be a widespread bias against good
documentation, particularly on the part of professional
programmers.
I have a friend who manages a large computer
software development group, and after many years of
aggravation has finally solved the problem of getting the
programming staff to develop documentation. He makes
them complete the documentation before the first line of
coding is written.
One of the most important parts of the documentation
is the run instructions. In many situations, the
teachers, aides, or other personnel who will be assisting
students with the courseware will have very little
computer skill or knowledge. Therefore, the run
instructions must be very explicit, including even
information about operating the microcomputer that is not
unique to your courseware. The reputation of a piece of
computer software, as it is used (or misused) in the
hands of minimally skilled people, can hinge on some
pretty minor points.

The Subject Matter

One of the most difficult things to assess quickly
is the subject matter of the CAI lesson. Most CAI
courseware is not even accompanied by so much as an
outline of the lesson content. However, if you have done
a conscientious, systems-based lesson development, your
process documents give you the basis for representing

this information, and the attributes of your work can be readily communicated and appreciated.

Relationship to Other Curricular Materials

If the relationship of your material to other curricular materials has been thought out and can be shared with prospective adopters, you will be able to provide a valuable service and enhance the usefulness of your courseware immensely.

The Intended Population

In all adoption decisions, the appropriateness of the material for the intended audience is a major consideration. Unfortunately, this is one of the hardest kinds of information to obtain. You will give your lesson a big advantage if you have conducted your validation with an appropriate student population and if you communicate that fact to the prospective adopters.

The Run Environment

Most adopters are probably "locked in" to a particular microcomputer. They set out to find courseware that will run on their "environment," rather than selecting courseware and then purchasing the microcomputer that will run it. This fact is important to you as a CAI author. It means that you should write for the microcomputer most widely used by the group which you expect will use your courseware. Ideally, you should prepare multiple versions of your lessons to run on different microcomputers and even on different models of the same microcomputer.

Your documentation should include information on all aspects of the run environment. I will list and discuss some of the main aspects here, but the guideline is to communicate fully any information the potential adopter will need to make a decision.

The Microcomputer

In almost all brands of microcomputers, there has been a succession of new models already. In some cases software and courseware written for earlier versions of microcomputers will run on subsequent versions, and in some cases it will not. Unfortunately, you can not always count on the vendor or even the manufacturer to tell you that. Some manufacturers are particularly callous if the software in question was not released by them.

Therefore, it is incumbent on you to be very specific about the microcomputer models which your courseware will run on. If modifications to the hardware are required, include that fact in your documentation.

Memory Size

In many school environments the decision has been made to purchase microcomputers with a minimum amount of memory, either to save money, or more likely, in order to maximize the number of microcomputers which could be purchased with a fixed amount of money. At any rate the minimum memory size needed to run a particular piece of courseware is a critical measure in deciding upon adoption.

Peripherals

Another very important consideration is the peripherals required, such as tape drives, disk drives, printers, and so forth. Again, because many schools have attempted to conserve funds, there often is a lack of peripherals in the field. At any rate, it must be specified if peripherals are required. This is especially true if anything unusual or exotic, such as a speech synthesizer, is required.

Hardware Modifications

Some courseware requires the use of special hardware (or "firmware") modifications, such as language cards. This fact must be conveyed to the potential users as well.

Software Required

Some courseware may require the presence of additional, sometimes nonstandard, software in order to run. The author has a responsibility to include this in the documentation of the lesson.

Auxiliary Equipment Required

Some courseware is now being written so that it will control the presentation of adjunctive material on a videotape recorder or videodisc player. The availability of such equipment can well be the determining factor in the adoption of such a lesson.

The Size of the Lesson

The size of a lesson can be very important to a teacher, or anyone considering the adoption of a CAI lesson, and yet one almost never sees it mentioned in a review. There is no standardized way of indicating the size of a lesson, either. Perhaps the most frequent measure is the maximum size of random access memory (RAM) required by the lesson. This tells someone how big the computer memory must be. However, it does not indicate how big the lesson is because the lesson could be segmented and the memory filled many different times.

What the teacher really wants to know is: "How long, on the average, can I expect my students to require to complete the lesson?" To answer such a question requires validation data, and since very few lessons are validated, it is no wonder that this information is seldom, if ever, supplied.

The teacher also needs to know, if the lesson is quite large, whether or not the lesson is segmented so that students can be assigned lessons in reasonable sized pieces. Another reasonable measure would be the number of question frames or student responses required.

The Conditions of Use

Of major concern to a teacher is the degree of independence the student will have as he or she works on the lesson. Ideally, the student should be able to take the courseware to a microcomputer, start the machine, load the lesson, and work independently until finished, at which point the teacher might come by and record the student's progress. It would be even better if the student's progress record was stored on the lesson medium so that the teacher could monitor it at any time that was convenient.

Furthermore, the lesson should permit the student to stop the lesson at any time and then should return him or her to the correct point in the lesson whenever he or she comes back to it.

Unfortunately, few CAI lessons are this self-instructional. More likely, the student will summon the teacher for assistance many times during the lesson, and the help needed may not be that obvious or easy to give. The student progress will not be stored permanently, and therefore the teacher may have to be there when the student finishes to record the scores from the screen before the machine is turned off and it is lost forever. And don't ask what happens when there is a power failure.

The Cost

The cost of the courseware can be a very complex thing that bears very careful examination. The initial cost may be for one copy of the lesson with unlimited privileges to copy it within the same organization. More likely, each additional copy must be bought, but at a reduced rate. Occasionally, courseware is licensed to an institution for a finite period of time at a single fee.

One of the neatest methods I have seen is a vendor who sells the first copy and then sells a sheet of contact labels at a small fee per label. The labels are professionally printed, and state that the copy is a legally prepared copy. As the vendor puts it, "It makes us both feel better." One of the nicest features of this technique is that you can comfortably regenerate copies that get damaged; and believe me, when you work with students discs will get damaged.

Some vendors, in their zeal to avoid having copies "ripped off" go to great lengths to make it difficult (they hope impossible) to copy their materials. In most cases, you are expected to return any damaged courseware to their national headquarters, usually pay a fee, and then wait and wait for the courseware to be returned to you. In the meantime, you are without the courseware. Some otherwise good courseware is not successful because of penurious policies such as this.

It should be noted that such policies are the equivalent of a dare to some programmers I have known who delight in cracking the codes and copying such software just to prove they can do it.

Expendable Materials Required?

Often times, auxiliary material (particularly expendable, or consumable, material which gets used up) can greatly increase the cost of using a CAI lesson. One must be sure to look into the cost and continued availabilty of such material before making an adoption decision.

Record Keeping

It is important that courseware keep a record of the student's performance. At a minimum, the courseware should provide for tallying the number of errors the student makes. Most courseware provides only this minimum feature, and some courseware doesn't even do that.

At the next level, the courseware should keep track of exactly which items are missed, and better yet, be able to provide a listing of the incorrect responses the student makes. It is desirable if the courseware stores the information on the disk or cassette so that the teacher can review the student's progress at any time. Unfortunately, most courseware does not maintain the information on disk or cassette, and the teacher must be on hand to record the information from the screen by hand. If the teacher fails to do this, and the machine is turned off, the information is simply lost. The same thing happens, of course, if the power fails.

In a really good record-keeping system, the information is kept on the disk or cassette, and the courseware is able to keep track of the student's place in the lesson, so that if a student is off the system for a while, he or she can be returned to the right place when signing back on.

QUALITY CONSIDERATIONS

All of the considerations made up to this point deal with describing the physical characteristics of the lesson, rather than with evidence or even value judgments of the quality of the lesson. The areas which we will now discuss are less obvious characteristics, but have a great deal to do with the success and effectiveness of the lesson.

It should always be borne in mind that the single most important factor in determining the quality of any instructional product is how well it works. It makes little sense to criticize the specific details of a CAI lesson that works excellently. The best evidence of the excellence of courseware is validation data. A few, generally professionally developed examples of courseware are accompanied by a record of the validation process.

However, it is rare that really excellent, validated courseware is encountered. Rather, most of the CAI courseware one is likely to see, at least for the immediate future, will require careful critiquing.

Instructional Design

A major consideration in evaluating the quality of a CAI lesson is the instructional design chosen and its appropriateness to the subject matter of the lesson. A great many of the people authoring CAI courseware for microcomputers are not well versed in the variety of lesson designs that are possible, and therefore don't have the freedom to select optimum lesson designs to fit a large variety of lesson content.

Frame Design

The same thing that was just said about lesson design is probably even more true of frame design. Most current CAI authors do not have enough variety of frame styles in their repertoires and also lack the facility with instructional technology to match frame style to frame purpose.

Interaction

Related to faulty frame design is the issue of insufficient interaction between the student and the computer. What usually results is a failure to fully exploit the range of capabilities of the computer. Even people who are not very conversant with the intricacies of CAI sense, and rightly so, that the interactive capabilities of the computer should be employed fully.

I have often witnessed a sort of "cop out" on the part of people who were negative about CAI, or who, while positive about CAI, had produced lessons which were less than optimally interactive. This is to deny that interactiveness is all that desirable, or, to deny that it is desirable in the case at hand. The weight of the evidence is very much against those whose policy it is to play down interaction, and I suspect that their "theory" about interaction is a "theory of convenience."

Response Economy

One of the things that is easy to spot in evaluating a CAI lesson is response economy. Does the author require the student to make laborious, time-consuming responses that do not add to the pedagogical effectiveness of the lesson? Could more economical reponse modes be used to accomplish the same learning?

Writing Style

Much of the value of a CAI lesson is determined by the effectiveness of the instructional writing found within it. Nothing will cause students to lose respect for a lesson as quickly as spelling errors or obvious grammatical errors such as the lack of agreement between subject and verb.

When teachers use a CAI lesson in class, they inherit the responsibility for any shortcomings the lesson may have. Few teachers would want to endure for long the embarrassment that badly written material can cause.

Directions

The CAI lesson must include directions that enable the student to know at all times exactly what is expected of him or her. The student should be given a simple way of signaling to the computer that he or she is lost and needs additional help. The teacher should not have to come and "rescue" the student.

Readability

There are two important aspects to readability. One has to do with the grade level that the lesson is intended for. The second has to do with the consideration the writer has for the comfort and welfare of the reader, regardless of the grade level. Both should be considered when evaluating a CAI lesson.

Spelling

One of the most unforgivable faults that can occur in a CAI lesson is spelling errors. Spelling errors are unforgivable because they are so easy to correct on a microcomputer. They are so obvious, even to the untrained reviewer. Spelling errors are a dead giveaway that the lesson has not been so much as proofread, let alone validated.

Grammar

Grammatical errors are also easy to correct on a microcomputer and are therefore unacceptable in a CAI lesson that is offered for sale. There may be times when there is an apparent conflict between the instructional requirements of the lesson and good grammatical usage. The author who opts for instructional effectiveness over grammatical rules should not be condemned. Remember that the rules of grammar exist to facilitate communication, not the other way around.

Instructional Language Usage

One of the secrets of an effective lesson is the way in which it makes use of instructional language techniques. A good CAI lesson should show considerable evidence of figurative language, mnemonics and other pedagogical devices.

Format

The frames of a good CAI lesson should show variety and should be well matched to the purpose of the lesson. The frames should be relatively uncrowded, and the line breaks should be properly placed.

Distribution of Emphasis

How well the resources of the lesson are distributed among the topics being taught is an important measure of the lesson's quality. Does the author spend a lot of time, words, and questions on things that are rather obvious, and then in other parts of the lesson skip by topics that need and deserve much more thorough treatment? Unfortunately this is something that happens a great deal, in all forms of instructional delivery.

OPTIMUM USE OF THE COMPUTER

The microcomputer is a very powerful tool, one that is capable of many things that can benefit the instructional process. Unfortunately, many CAI lessons fail to exploit the microcomputer as fully as might be desired. In many cases, the computer is used as little more than an electronic page turner, or worse, electronic flashcards.

Reviewers typically have a computer background and spend a great deal of time looking at the way in which the computer is used. The manner in which automatic delays are built in to allow students time to read are often criticized for being too long or too short. A good way around this is to eliminate automatic timing loops, and put frame succession under the control of the student.

Currently, there is also a high value placed on the use of branching, often to the extent that "linear" programs are put down as not being worthy of use. I think this is a passing fad, and the value of each type of lesson design will come to be appreciated for the task it does best. At any rate, don't make the mistake of using branching inappropriately, just as an attempt to avoid this type of unfair criticism. In fact there are good reasons to avoid branching unless it serves a valid pedagogical purpose. A branching program is usually costlier to create and more difficult to validate and revise than a linear program which covers the same content.

I have included a sample review checklist here for your reference (fig. 10-1). It is somewhat more complete than those usually encountered, although there are additional things that could be included. No checklist can completely eliminate the need for a subjective, narrative component of the review.

Fig. 10-1

```
┌──────────────────────────────────────────────────────────┐
│            CAI COURSEWARE REVIEW CHECK LIST                │
└──────────────────────────────────────────────────────────┘

        ┌──────────────────────────────────────────┐
        │             USER INFORMATION             │
        └──────────────────────────────────────────┘
┌──────────────────────────────────────────────────────────┐
│ TITLE OF COURSEWARE:                                       │
├──────────────────────────────────────────────────────────┤
│ SUBJECT MATTER:                                            │
├──────────────────────────────────────────────────────────┤
│ AUTHOR:                                                    │
├──────────────────────────────────────────────────────────┤
│ PUBLISHER:                                                 │
├──────────────────────────────────────────────────────────┤
│ DISTRIBUTOR:                                               │
├──────────────────────────────────────────────────────────┤
│ PRICE:           BACKUPS:            COST:                 │
└──────────────────────────────────────────────────────────┘

        ┌──────────────────────────────────────────┐
        │            ENVIRONMENT REQUIRED          │
        └──────────────────────────────────────────┘
┌──────────────────────────────────────────────────────────┐
│ MICROCOMPUTER:                                             │
├──────────────────────────────────────────────────────────┤
│ MEMORY:                                                    │
├──────────────────────────────────────────────────────────┤
│ PERIPHERALS:                                               │
├──────────────────────────────────────────────────────────┤
│ HARDWARE MODIFICATIONS:                                    │
├──────────────────────────────────────────────────────────┤
│ SOFTWARE:                                                  │
├──────────────────────────────────────────────────────────┤
│ AUXILIARY EQUIPMENT:                                       │
└──────────────────────────────────────────────────────────┘
```

Fig.10-1 (continued)

LESSON SIZE

AVERAGE COMPLETION TIME:
NUMBER OF DISCS /TAPES:
AMOUNT OF MEMORY:
NUMBER OF QUESTION FRAMES:
NUMBER OF SEGMENTS:

RECORD KEEPING

NO RECORD KEEPING OF ANY KIND:
TALLY OF INCORRECT RESPONSES:
LISTING OF INCORRECT RESPONSES:
RECORD OF PERFORMANCE STORED ON DISK OR CASSETTE:
STUDENT IS RETURNED TO PLACE WHEN SIGNING BACK ON:
STUDENT GRADE IS AUTOMATICALLY COMPUTED:

COMPUTER USAGE

BRANCHING ADEQUATE:
TIMED DELAYS ADEQUATE:
SPECIAL FEATURES WELL EXPLOITED:

Fig. 10-1 (continued)

VALIDATION DATA

NO VALIDATION DATA AVAILABLE:	INTENDED AUDIENCE:
NATURE OF VALIDATION POPULATION:	NUMBER:
CRITERION(A) AND PERFORMANCE:	

WRITING STYLE		

	INADEQUATE	ADEQUATE	EXCELLENT
DIRECTIONS			
READABILITY			
SPELLING			
GRAMMAR			
USAGE			
EMPHASIS			

LESSON DESIGN		

	INADEQUATE	ADEQUATE	EXCELLENT
FRAMES VARIED:			
APPROPRIATE:			
INTERACTION:			
RESPONSE ECONOMY:			
PREDOMINANT DESIGN:			

11

CASHING IN

There are a great many options open to the person who can author CAI courseware. They range from writing and selling your courseware on your own in your spare time to starting your own company of whatever size, to taking a position with a publisher or software production company. The more carefully you study the options, the more likely you are to choose a course that is right for you.

GETTING STARTED

Unless you have unlimited access to one of the more popular microcomputers, you should invest in your own very early. Ideally, it should be the one which is the most widely used by the student population for which you intend to develop lessons. It is also very convenient if it can be the same as microcomputers that you may have at work. I own a system which is exactly the same as some of the equipment I have at work, and it is very convenient. It allows me to continue projects at noon and in the mornings before work, whenever I manage to get in early enough. Unfortunately, it also tempts you to take work home.

Although the initial purchase price may represent a major investment for you, it will allow you to make better use of your time and I'm certain it will turn out to be a good investment.

PUBLISHING AND DISTRIBUTING YOUR OWN COURSEWARE

One of the easiest ways to get started is to create a useful CAI lesson which you think will be purchased, and place an ad in a national magazine. Some of the many magazines devoted to microcomputers have very reasonable rates considering their wide but selective coverage.

Have your paper documentation prepared so that you can run it off on your own printer. Lay in a supply of the plastic bags with the "zip top" closure which are large enough to hold your lesson medium and the documentation. Obtain some sturdy mailing envelopes and some heavy cardboard for stiffening.

When the orders arrive, duplicate your lessons on the correct medium, verify them, pack them up, and send them out. As you can see, the investment and the risk are both minimal.

While this is a good way to get started, you will soon want to investigate other means of distributing your work, particularly if you are a prolific CAI lesson producer. Many inventors or small manufacturers have destroyed their opportunity for real success by trying to hang onto all the pieces of their operation themselves. It is usually better to confine one's activity to the part one does best, and let other professionals do their part. By placing your materials with a large distributor who will take care of production as well as sales you can optimize your success. It is typically better to have a part of something big than all of something small.

GETTING PUBLISHED

Another approach is to think of the creation of CAI as somewhat the same thing as writing a book, and attempt to get it published by a regular publisher. Most of the large publishers and some new, small, specialty publishers are moving into the area of microcomputer CAI courseware production, and publishing very rapidly. In most cases, they are just finding their way. Pricing, and royalty rates are still very much in a state of flux. Most of the publishers are proceeding cautiously, and with a great concern for the quality of the work. The one thing you can probably be sure of is getting a good audience when you talk to them.

Contracts

The best approach is probably to proceed just as one would if writing a book. First, put together a proposal which describes the intended project. Most publishers even have forms for book proposals, and much of the information called for will likely apply to CAI courseware as well.

There are some obvious differences between books and CAI courseware, however, that necessitate some precautions. Make sure, for example, that if the lesson is adapted for microcomputers other than the one you have written it for, that you still get your royalty.

Royalties

Generally speaking royalties are on a sliding scale. On a book, for instance, they are typically 10 percent on the first ten thousand copies and 15 percent thereafter. This reflects the fact that a publishing firm usually has to have a certain volume of sales before it begins to show a profit, often as much as $200,000. This is because of the front loading of development and advertising costs.

Although publishers are still finding their way in this field, if you work with a major publisher, you can be confident that you will be treated fairly. Publishers have a vested interest in preserving the traditions as well as the laws with respect to the author's property rights as represented by his or her written products.

COURSEWARE WRITTEN UNDER CONTRACT

Another way to approach the writing of CAI is to find an organization which needs custom-written CAI courseware. Many corporations have training departments which regularly contract with "outside consultants" to provide a variety of services, including the writing of CAI materials.

There are distinct advantages to writing CAI courseware under contract. One is that you know there is a market for your work, and since the clients have an immmediate need, they are likely to be willing to pay well. Often, they can justify the cost as a proportion of the savings possible using your materials versus using live instruction. Usually, the money that is saved by eliminating travel and per diem costs is more than enough to justify what they pay you.

A second advantage has to do with the time frame. You will usually have to commit to a specific deadline, meaning that you will usually finish the project sooner than if you had no deadline. You will most likely be paid in full upon delivery. Although that may be all the money you ever receive for the project, you are reasonably sure of the money. Lessons written on speculation or for royalties are more of a gamble, and the returns can be very disappointing when you finally realize them.

SEEKING A JOB AS A CAI AUTHOR

If you get to the point where you feel you want to write CAI courseware full time, and you want the security of a full-time job rather than working for yourself, you have that option. More and more publishers are setting up CAI courseware production units. You will probably have to be prepared to move unless you already live in one of the few parts of the country where large publishers are located.

It is probably best to start with the large publishers, since with them, you will more than likely find that you can specialize in CAI authorship exclusively, rather than having to wear several hats. You are also more likely to find a career ladder of sorts which will allow you upward mobility, at least in salary.

Be careful that you do not have to sign away your right to produce your own lessons "on the side." You should be able to do this so long as your personal products don't compete directly with those you are producing at work.

There are several advantages to be gained from working for a large company. One of these is colleagueship. You can learn a great deal from your peers. Some writing environments provide an intellectual environment which is more stimulating than many academic environments.

Another advantage is that you become part of a national network and may be able to travel quite a lot, particularly to conventions and trade shows. This is an excellent way to stay current in your field. Many companies also provide an excellent library of books and periodicals, unavailable in almost any other organization.

As you can see, there are many opportunities open to the individual who can author CAI courseware. No doubt there are numerous other options that have not been mentioned here. My main point in including this chapter is to help you to be aware of some of these options, and hopefully, to inspire you to become involved in this exciting opportunity.

12

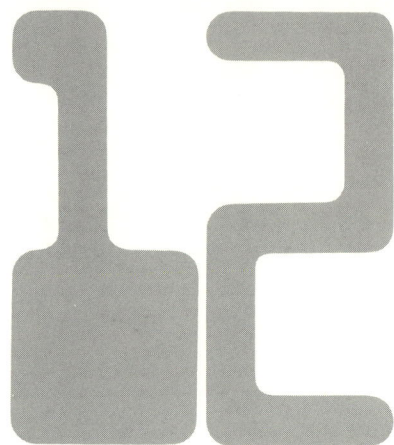

THE FUTURE OF MICROCOMPUTER CAI

Lest you think I am interested only in past and present models of CAI design, I would like to use this last chapter to take a brief flight of fancy and consider what the future of CAI might be like. I realize that this is a dangerous endeavor in a field where the half-

170

life of most ideas is probably much less than five years and decreasing every day.

HARDWARE DEVELOPMENTS WE CAN EXPECT

It is developments in the hardware of computers that spawned the microcomputer revolution — specifically, in the manufacturing methods which made the electronic components of the hardware cheaper, smaller, and more tolerable of ambient conditions. However, some of the mechanical components of the computer have actually increased in price, due to inflation. The only thing likely to bring down the cost of the mechanical part of the computer is volume of sales and competition.

Therefore, the cost of basic computers is not likely to come down much more. However, we are likely to see tremendous increases in the features of microcomputers and in the reliability. These will result from further miniaturization and further exploitation of the low cost of manufacturing the electronic components.

The increase in reliability will be a result of improved materials and methods, of course, but it will also result from something else — redundancy. Circuits will be created in which there are backup components which duplicate key elements of the circuit — perhaps several times. In that way, if the first component in a set of identical components is bad at the time of first use or goes bad at any time, a redundant component in the set will take over, and so forth. If this technique is well exploited, electronic equipment failures will become rare indeed.

The low cost of microcomputers has created a large and very diverse user group. As a result, people are constantly finding new applications for microcomputers. This results in a demand for an ever increasing variety of hardware modifications.

One of the microcomputer hardware features that is overdue for replacement is the cathode ray tube, or CRT. As the last remaining vacuum tube in an all solid state device, and right out there in front like it is, it is a conspicuous anachronism. Given all the attention it has been given lately as a potential health hazard, particularly for those who use a CRT all day every day, it is an especially good candidate for replacement.

The most likely replacement technology for the CRT is some sort of liquid crystal device. Some manufacturers have been teasing us by showing small prototypes of such a display at trade shows. Another likely area for development in displays is laser technology. I think it's only a matter of time until new technology emerges to replace the familiar cathode ray tube as a microcomputer display device. Whatever is developed will have to meet simultaneous demands for safety, cost and aesthetics.

Certainly keyboards are another area in which there is room for improvement. The ones we are using now are basically a descendent of the mechanical typewriter. The key movement was once necessary to create mechanical action in a typebar linkage. That is no longer needed. All we need to do now is close a switch to create a letter on the screen. There may be better ways yet to come.

There are experimental keyboards under development within many organizations, some of which are based on advanced concepts of ergonomics. Even a smaller keyboard, better suited to the hands of children, would be an improvement.

The whole issue of keyboards may become much less important in the not too distant future if the current development of voice recognition and comprehension techniques continues. The current problem is not recognition, but comprehension — comprehension even to the level of producing simple transcriptions of what is spoken. Even the largest, fastest, mainframe computers can take up to an hour to transcribe a single sentence at present. And even then the sentence is only approximately 90 percent accurate.

However, given the present rate of development, there is every reason to be optimistic. Given the adequate development of this technology, we will be able to produce CAI lessons that are totally aural and visual, and that accept oral input. I think that this kind of conversational mode will make the role of the student much more pleasant. I also think the work of the CAI author will be lightened as well.

Most microcomputers still plug into the wall, which limits their portability. Speaking as one who has probably spent hundreds of hours lugging microcomputers to and from workshops, classes, and demonstrations of all sorts, current microcomputers are not **really** all that portable. The main power users in a microcomputer are the CRT and the tape or disc drives. If these two technologies undergo the development that I anticipate they will, microcomputers will become much more portable.

We read constantly about new memory devices with tremendously increased storage capacities in smaller and smaller spaces. One must be particularly cautious in this area, since there have been many promising memory devices, for example, that have not made it into production for one reason or another. However, one can be certain that where there is a demand, there will eventually be a satisfier for that demand.

The benefits of increased storage capacity which is economical will be very great for CAI. Many of the most attractive applications are not cost effective, or even possible on today's microcomputers. An example is very high resolution graphics.

Many current microcomputers are capable of communicating with each other and with larger computers. However, given the communications equipment, specifically the modems which are priced appropriately for microcomputer use, the rate of communication is very slow. As a result, the communication lines are not used efficiently, and few people are able to afford the line cost.

I think we can expect great improvements in communications equipment along with cost reductions. We can probably also look forward to reductions in the tariff rates for data transmission. The result will be that communication via microcomputers will increase, and there will be a tremendous impact on education as a result.

We are beginning to see the use of "information utilities" designed primarily for microcomputer users. As educational resources, information utilities offer a great deal of promise, placing a vast amount of the world's information (in the form of data bases) within reach of any classroom with a microcomputer, a modem, and a telephone.

SOFTWARE DEVELOPMENTS WE CAN EXPECT

While there will continue to be a considerable amount of change in microcomputer hardware, there will be much more change by far in the software area. The software development area has lagged far behind the hardware area. In many applications areas, we are only very belatedly beginning to see reasonable software. There is a lot more potential to be tapped in the state-of-the-art microcomputer.

One of the things we can expect is for the hardware to become much more "invisable" to the software. That is, software will be created which will run on a much wider variety of microcomputers than is currently the case.

We can also expect the "friendliness" trend to continue. Software, and to some extent hardware, will become more tolerant of user errors, will "interpret" user intentions from a wider range of user actions, and will offer more on-line user guidance and support.

It will become easier to modify software to user requirements and taste than has been the case. The word processing software that I am using to write this book, for example, permits me to modify it so that the options I prefer come up automatically as I load it. For example, I do not like to hyphenate, so the hyphenation option comes up in the "off" mode. I like double spacing, so that now comes up; similarly, the "insertion" mode. These may seem like small things, but they are important to anyone who spends a significant portion of each day (and night) writing.

COMPUTER ASSISTANCE FOR CAI AUTHORS

Probably the thing that will have the greatest impact on the CAI field in the immediate future is the further development of CAI authoring systems which speed up the creation of CAI courseware. We have discussed the first generation of such systems earlier in the book.

The second generation of such systems are already available. They are much more expensive than the first generation, but they are also more capable. They permit the use of a much wider variety of CAI lesson designs.

As capable as the second generation of CAI authoring systems is, the second generation is still only a beginning. I think we are likely to see assistance for the CAI author which will help with all phases of the development process, from front-end analysis to validation and revision.

For example, it is not too difficult to conceive of a system which would lead the CAI author through the development of a topic list, through the task list, task analysis, and the creation of learning objectives. Following and building on that, it would help with the sequencing of the materials and with the selection of a lesson design, and then produce a flow chart automatically.

The construction of the lesson would be greatly assisted by the computer as well, many parts, such as the creation of a record-keeping system, being completely automatic. The spelling, vocabulary, and other aspects of writing style would be checked automatically as well.

Finally, the validation process would be planned and controlled automatically as well. In short, the computer would be the most helpful with those mechanical tasks which we all know are important, but which we tend to neglect.

The payoff for all of this will be the existence of lots of good inexpensive CAI courseware — inexpensive because it will be less labor intensive to produce than is now the case.

I think CAI authoring systems will continue to evolve and be improved. Among the improvements that I expect to see are a variety of authoring aids, such as an on-line dictionary, thesaurus, and monitoring for such features as readability and reading grade level.

NEW MODELS OF CAI

Most of the developments we have discussed so far have dealt with the improvement of methods of producing traditional CAI courseware. However, one of the things we can already see happening, and which will almost certainly continue, is the diversification of models of CAI.

In part, this is a result of large numbers of people with varied backgrounds creating CAI lessons. Many of these people have backgrounds, values, and philosophies which are very different from those of the pioneers of the CAI movement. While there is great variability in the lessons produced and in the designs used, much of it is quite good. Out of this mix will come a lot of creative new ideas about exactly what constitutes CAI. The result will be some permanent contributions to the development of the concept of CAI.

UNOBTRUSIVE INSTRUCTIONAL SYSTEMS

One of the problems with most of the models of CAI that have been developed so far is that they are very unnatural and inefficient. The process of asking students questions to test their understanding may be putting the cart before the horse. It might be more logical and a better pedagogical ploy to have the student ask the questions and have the system answer them.

There are several obvious and not so obvious reasons why we now do it the other way around. One is that "that is the way we have traditionally done it." In traditional, group-paced instructional environments, it is necessary, for the sake of coordination and efficiency, to have all of the students do the same thing at the same time. Questioning provides the instructional system with the controlling function.

Another important reason for the system questioning the student rather than the other way around is that there must be a record of the students learning for certification purposes. System-originated questions together with answers provided by the student constitute such a record.

Finally, what would now constitute a sufficient reason by itself even if the reasons cited above were overcome, is that given the state of the art in computing, it would be next to impossible to arrange for the computer to understand the questions. That problem will be overcome eventually, I am sure, and at that time, the computer will also be able to respond to students questions.

The lesson strategy then will be to teach students the skills of inquiry. Certification of learning will no doubt still be necessary, but it can just as well be based on a record of the students inquiry activities. Hopefully, there will evolve a refined process of structuring data bases, in such a way that students will be rewarded for following good inquiry methods.

REMOTE-SENSING CAI

Many people learn very well on their own. Most people, even those who have attained a high level of formal education, have learned a great deal of what they know by personal study rather than by study within a formal educational setting. The problem with such learning is that it is difficult to be certain that it has taken place, and therefore it is difficult to receive social recognition for it.

It would be nice if there was a way of monitoring such learning and recognizing it. The conventional methods of measuring learning, like testing and measuring the time spent in formal courses, are "obtrusive" methods. That means that time spent in certifying learning actually takes time and effort away form the learning activities themselves.

Wouldn't it be better to find a way of certifying learning that is unobtrusive? The computer may provide some solutions in this matter.

One technology that holds promise for this is remote-sensing technology. NASA has developed high altitude remote sensing to a very sophisticated, reliable level. The same principles and some of the same techniques can be applied to the monitoring of a learner to assess, to a large extent without interfering with the learning activities, whether or not learning is taking place.

The main instrumentation for such an endeavor would be an **occulometer**. An occulometer can be used to monitor the direction of the gaze of the eyes, as well as pupil diameter. Other instruments which could be used would include biofeedback-type instrumentation for monitoring such things as respiration rate, heart rate, galvanic skin response, muscle activity, and brain wave activity.

Infrared imaging could be used to look at such things as facial blood flow patterns — a concomitant of affect and emotional state. Voice stress analysis could be used for somewhat the same purpose for spoken responses.

Suppose that a student is directed to simply read narrative text on a computer display such as a CRT. Suppose further that the remote-sensing instrumentation mentioned above is able to simultaneously monitor all relavant measures of student learning behavior.

The software techniques needed to synthesize the data are similar to those developed by NASA to enhance images taken by satellite telemetry. As the scientists

176

who work on such things put it, such software "learns" to see more and more as additional kinds of corroborative data become available to it.

At the simplest level, the computer can be used to monitor eye movements to determine if students are moving their eyes in a pattern that could indicate that they are reading — that is, students eyes are moving along each line, from left to right, and from top to bottom. In addition the system could be used to monitor attentional state and brain wave activity to see that there is cognitive activity going on.

At a more sophisticated level, the material could be edited to determine where memory loading, problem-solving effort, and insight should occur. There is considerable experimental evidence that indicates that this is possible. This editorial technique, while somewhat time consuming, is far easier than authoring CAI courseware.

When more computer power is available, the material can be automatically edited on a normative basis. As large numbers of students read through the materials, the patterns derived should indicate automatically what the ideal patterns of physiological measures should be. The longer the system is used, the larger the data base will be, and the better its ability to analyze any single student's pattern.

COMPUTER ENVIRONMENTS

The computer changes any environment in which it is used. A computer is brought into an accounting department, for example, and the accounting department is never quite the same. The same is true when a computer is brought into a classroom. Things are possible in that classroom that never were possible before.

The computer can be used to deliberately change an environment in certain ways, to make new things possible. For example, a computer can be used to connect a classroom in to national information networks. A classroom so connected is different in a substantive way than a classroom which is not.

If we use a very broad definition of CAI such as I suggested in chapter 2 — namely, that CAI is the direct use of the computer to facilitate and certify learning — then some exciting new things are already happening in an area referred to as "computer environments."

An Environment for Learning to Write

The microcomputer can be made to function as a **word processing system**. That is, with the addition of the proper software, it can be made to operate as an "intelligent, electronic typewriter." As manuscripts are

177

keyed into the microcomputer, carriage returns are done automatically by the microcomputer as is pagination, and the manuscript is stored on a diskette. The manuscript can then be printed from the diskette at any time, and as many times as desired.

Depending on the microcomputer, the software, and the printer used, the copy can be printed out in a form that is acceptable for offset printing. If a carbon film ribbon is used, and the copy is justified in both margins with proportional spacing, the output is beautiful indeed.

The real time-saving features and the thing that endears microcomputer word processing to the hearts of all writers who are fortunate enough to have it available to them is the great convenience of editing and revision that it provides. Increases in productivity from initial writing to final version are estimated variously by many writers to be between two to ten times that of standard typing methods.

Most writers who have turned to microcomputer word processing have been prepared for the increase in productivity. What they did not anticipate was the extent to which it improves the writing ability of even veteran writers.

Now, imagine an environment for teaching writing in which **each** student has unlimited access to the best available microcomputer word processor. In other words, each individual in the class has his or her own personal unit, including a printer. I believe that the creation of such an environment would stimulate the creation of a new and highly effective methodology for teaching and learning the art of writing.

The ease of writing, and particularly of revision, would create an environment in which teachers were not reluctant to ask for any kind of revision, major or minor, and students would not be at all resentful. I think that teachers would find that students were much more productive, and much less refractory to instruction.

This environment could be further enhanced by the addition of some writing aids, some of which are already available, and some of which will very likely be available soon. For example, there are already computerized dictionaries, which can be loaded into a microcomputer and automatically check the spelling of the written material. A thesaurus would be another helpful addition.

One can easily conceive of additional aids to writers, such as perhaps a system which would accept bibliographic information in menu driven format and yield either footnotes or a bibliography, properly alphabetized, in any one of several standard formats. Of course, one of the outcomes that is certain to result from working in such an environment is the invention of additional aids that occur to no one now.

A Learning Environment Which Brings the World to the Classroom

National computer communication networks have already been established which can be accessed by any one of several standard microcomputers, through a simple, inexpensive piece communications gear (called a modem) over a standard telephone line. A one-time only subscription fee is usually required, and then the user is billed monthly at a very nominal rate for connect time and storage if applicable.

At the heart of the system is usually a bank of minicomputers. There are many services available from the network center itself. However, the unique value of the network is the opportunity it presents to create a specialized learning environment within a classroom.

Suppose that a classroom were set up with a microcomputer which was connected to the network. It would make a wide variety of information sources, ranging from the wire service to the Big Board of the stock market available within the classroom. It would be delightful to see what could result within such an environment, populated by a creative teacher and an able class.

There are already many other environments which could be described and many others which could be imagined. Certainly, many more will be created. Hardly a week goes by that one does not hear of yet another new microcomputer application, often simply a new way of applying an established system. The beautiful thing is that there are so many people using microcomputers in so many creative ways — ways that computer professionals such as computer engineers and systems designers, would most likely never have thought of. "May The Force be with them."

A GLOSSARY OF CAI TERMS

ABOUT THE GLOSSARY

The CAI field is made up of people with very diverse backgrounds. There is great variability in the amount and type of training as well as experience among the current range of CAI authors. Therefore, there is considerable variability in the use of terms. There is, in fact, a "Tower of Babel" effect.

The purpose of the glossary is to help reduce this problem by explaining some of the terms used, and the concepts which the terms represent.

The CAI author is in an unusual position. He or she has the responsibility of making a computer simulate the actions of a human tutor, indeed, in some ways a superhuman tutor. The hardware of computing is evolving at a spectacular rate. There is little reason to think that anything we might reasonably want to do on a computer is impossible or will remain impossible for long. It's as someone said recently about science fiction, "There is no longer any such thing as science fiction. There are just things Man has not done yet."

The potential of the computer for direct instructional use is limited only by our imaginations. In the face of this profound potential, the CAI author is like a scientist without a science; an artist without an art. There is as yet, no single community of CAI scholars; no guild. There is no unified knowledge base for CAI authors.

Some of the material that might form a body of knowledge exists. It is, however, scattered among very diverse sources. To discover all this information would require a considerable amount of time and careful scholarship.

It is intended that this glossary, as well as the previous parts of this book, will bring some of this information together in one place, in a manageable form. The format used is somewhat like a glossary or an encyclopedia. It is organized by terms and concepts, alphabetically. Each term is defined. Where necessary, further explanations are made and examples given. In many cases the relevance of the term to CAI is explained.

Some of the general sources of information are worthy of discussion at this time in order to orient the reader.

The field of psychology is in some senses the parent science of education and training. In effect, CAI then becomes a sort of applied psychology. Therefore, it is reasonable to draw on the considerable body of knowledge developed by learning theorists and researchers in both human and animal learning.

The programmed instruction movement was a particularly successful case of applied psychology. The experience and the literature of programmed instruction is an extremely rich source of information for CAI authors. Many of the people who participated in the PI movement were psychologists who took what they were doing very seriously. Much of their work was very well evaluated and documented in a sizable literature. Many of the concepts and techniques which were developed are quite adaptable to CAI.

Many PI practitioners were able to move on to CAI on large mainframe computers which, even though expensive to use, were subsidized in various ways and for various reasons. Probably all computer manufacturers maintained at least small-scale CAI projects as part of their research and development efforts. Some manufacturers, such as IBM, use CAI extensively for internal training purposes. In such cases, cost effectiveness is not an issue since they "own the candy store." The military has ongoing CAI training which is felt to be cost-justified because of distances involved, the sophistication of the training, or time constraints. The people involved in this activity have accumulated many years of experience in CAI, and even though it is with large, mainframe computers, their knowledge is quite adaptable to microcomputers.

There are other, less obviously relevant fields that nevertheless have considerable relevance to CAI. Teacher training, rhetoric, formal logic, and of course computer science are some of these.

Finally, there is the young but rapidly growing field of microcomputer CAI itself. New, relevant articles appear every month in the many periodicals devoted to microcomputers.

It is hoped therefore that this glossary will be of assistance as you collect your personal body of knowledge from these many sources.

GLOSSARY

Acronym An acronym is an artificial word usually made up of the first letter of each major word in a series of words. It is particularly useful to use as a mnemonic device when there is very little else to serve as a basis for the association of the items. An acronym can serve a useful purpose as a formal prompt as well.

Adaptive program A program which appears to "learn from experience." The program is designed so that each time it runs or receives new data, it uses the information gained to improve it's own approach. Some chess-playing programs are adaptive programs. When they are first run, a novice player may be able to beat them. After they have played many, many times, a world-class chess player may have great difficulty beating them.

Advance organizer In general, this concept is probably taken by most practitioners to mean any instructional strategy used in advance of the actual instruction to help the learner relate what he or she is about to learn to the knowledge he or she already possesses. Used in that sense, the concept can be quite useful to the CAI author.

Algorithm In its simplest meaning, an algorithm is a set of steps to be followed to accomplish a known result. Sometimes, however, it is used to refer to a set of steps that has the capacity for self-modification based on operating experience. Algorithms can be used in several different ways in CAI. They can be used to organize lessons and can serve as a mnemonic device for "tasky" kinds of learning.

Alliteration A concept from literature which involves the juxtaposition of words which begin with the same letter. The CAI author can use this device as a formal prompt, as a mnemonic device, and perhaps in other ways as well.

Alternative choice A term applied to a class of frame-types in which the student is expected to choose the correct answer from among a group of alternative

distractors, or wrong answers. Multiple-choice frames
and true-or-false frames are the main examples.

Ambiguity   When a **single** word or term can have two
or more distinct meanings it is said to be ambiguous.

Amphiboly   When a **group** of words or terms can have
two or more distinct meanings it is said to be
amphibolous. There are times amphiboly is intentional
and serves a good purpose, as is often the case in
poetry. However, it is much more often unintentional.
This is particularly true of textbooks, workbooks, and
CAI written for children. Careful analysis of almost any
didactic materials written for children will reveal a
multitude of these transgressions. Please be careful of
this in your own work.

Amplification   The didactic power of a lesson can
be increased by the skillful use of successively more
powerful didactic techniques. Each of these techniques
has both strengths and weaknesses, so their use involves
tradeoffs. Therefore it is necessary to use some kind of
empirical approach, combined with your own experience and
judgment, in the amplification of lessons.

Analogy   By drawing analogies between an item to
be learned and things the student is already likely to be
familiar with, learning and retention are likely to be
facilitated. The use of analogies may also increase the
likelihood that transfer of learning will occur. The
aphorism "All analogies limp" helps us to remember that
no analogy is perfect — that is, the two elements of the
analogy cannot be identical. Otherwise, it would not be
an analogy — by definition. In an analogy it is stated
explicitly that the thing to be learned "is like"
something else. Hopefully, the "something else" is
something the student is already familiar with.

Aphorism   Aphorisms have probably served a
didactic purpose for nearly as long as humankind has used
language. Don't hesitate to adopt or create aphorisms in
the service of your students and your lessons.

184

APPILOT   A version of the PILOT CAI authoring language, created specifically for the Apple II microcomputer.

APPLE ARISTOTLE   A test authoring system which also can function as a CAI authoring system.

Automated instruction   Any type of instruction, whose administration is controlled by an automated device, such as a teaching machine or a computer.

BABOON frames   A particularly useful type of frame in which the student is given a "A" choice and a "B" choice and can also choose "Both" or "Neither." The name BABOON is an acronym for B, A, BO(th), O(r) N(either). BABOON frames have the advantage of not prompting the student as much as simple "forced choice" items do.

Backup   For security reasons, it is good practice to create duplicate diskettes or cassettes of your software and courseware. The duplicates are referred to as backup copies.

BASIC   A widely used language for interactive, on-line programming whose name is an acronym for Beginner's All-Purpose Symbolic Instruction Code. It is patterned after FORTRAN and exists in many special dialects for different purposes and different computers. It also comes in various sizes with different numbers of instructions.

Bow-shaped-curve-of-retention   In serial list learning, it is customary to permit the learner to see the list, then test to see which items he or she recalls, repeating the process for a specified number of times, or until the list has been learned. When the retention results are plotted cumulatively, a "bow-shaped curve" almost always results. The implication of this for CAI authors is that material which occurs at the beginning, middle, and end of the lesson is learned earlier and is more likely to be retained. Material at the quarter point and at the three-quarter point is the slowest to be learned and least likely to be retained. A careful author will distribute critical items to be learned or retained accordingly.

Branching   In computer programming, branching refers to the practice of skipping to one of two or more points in the program, depending upon which one of a set of alternative conditions is met.

Branching program   Any program which uses built-in branching. Branching is usually designed to allow some students to bypass some of the material of the program based on their performance in the program to that point. It is now becoming fairly common to let the student branch based on his or her own choice or judgment. In that way, the student is allowed to participate in the management of instruction. Some types of branching programs are also called "intrinsic" or "Crowderian." Both terms are defined elsewhere in this glossary.

Chaining   In animal-conditioning experiments it is common practice to condition a chain of specific behaviors. It is done by conditioning the behaviors one at a time. Behavior A is first conditioned to a high level of habit strength. Then reinforcement is withheld unless the animal first performs behavior B as well. Then behaviors C, D, and so on are made preconditions in turn. The key is that the later the behavior is in the chain, the earlier it was conditioned. That's why it is sometimes called backward chaining. There are several practical implications of this for the instructional programmer. One is that it is often easier to design a program from back to front. One early instructional programmer became legendary, in part, for the way he designed lessons from right to left, filling blackboards or newsprint all the way around the room. Another implication is in something serial which has to be learned, such as poetry, a set of formulas, or the like. It might often make sense to begin with the final parts, and only add parts, working backward of course, after the last part has been learned well.

Clock   Inside a computer there are two main types of clocks. The first is simply a time-of-day clock. For some microcomputers, such as the Apple II, time-of-day clocks are available which are battery powered so they run even when the computer is turned off. These clocks can be used by the programmer in many ways, since the computer can, in effect, "read" the clock. The clock can be used to time lessons, response latencies, and other events. The clock can be used conditionally to control branching. It can also be used simply to print the time on reports.

The second type of clock controls the coordination of activity within the computer. To do this it must measure millionths of seconds. This clock is important since it determines, in part, the speed of the computer.

CMI   Computer managed instruction. Refers to any system in which a computer is used to perform overall instructional management. It usually includes a testing and evaluation function, a planning function, and a record-keeping function. All CAI has elements of CMI built in, but CMI usually refers to a more complete, stand-alone system.

Cognitive mapping   A technique in which the pattern of material is highly exploited in order to produce instructional efficiency and maximize transfer of learning. For example, when a set of items must be learned which have concepts in common, each concept may be taught only once and then merely referenced as each exemplar is taught. The term **cognitive mapping** is an allusion to an imaginary "map" of concepts cognitively layed over each exemplar with the indication of which concepts are relevant to it.

Its relevance in CAI is in great part as a time-saving technique. It might, for example, take the form of a check sheet to be filled in by the student for each exemplar to be learned. Some of the "outline" series used to assist students with basic college courses are excellent examples of the exploitation of this concept.

Cognitive style   Some people feel that there are distinct styles of thinking and thus of learning. They also feel that certain teaching-learning methodologies are better suited to one cognitive style than to another.

Computer assisted instruction   Any method of learning in which a computer is the primary delivery system. The definition has been narrowed somewhat, by tradition, so that for most people it probably means direct, interactive instruction in which the student is on-line to a computer.

187

Computer-based instruction   Nearly synonymous with CAI. However, some people may reserve the term CBI for cases in which there is less direct interaction with the computer.

Computer-managed instruction   CMI has come to mean the systematic control of instruction by the computer. It is characterized by testing, diagnosis, learning prescriptions, and thorough record keeping.

Computer-mediated instruction   A somewhat archaic term for computer-managed instruction or occasionally, even computer-assisted instruction.

Confusion matrix   In teaching a set of things in which the members of the set are like each other to various degrees, students may tend to confuse some members for certain others to varying degrees. Morse code is such an example. A table constructed to show the relative extent of confusion between each pair of symbols is called a **confusion matrix.** This concept is useful in CAI when one must manage such cases of potential negative transfer.

Constructed response   When, in responding to a question frame in CAI, students must spell out, calculate and supply, or otherwise "construct" an answer rather than choose it from alternatives given to them explicitly, they are said to be making a "constructed response."

Contingency management   Some psychologists feel that all, or nearly all, behavior is controlled by the consequences in the environment. These consequences are said to be contingencies of their respective behaviors. Much training, therefore, is thought of as "managing" the "contingencies" of behavior.

Convergent questioning   When a question is designed to narrow the field of discussion or study, it is called a convergent question.

Courseware   It has become popular to refer to CAI lessons as **courseware** rather than **software** as it has been traditionally called and technically is. This practice probably does aid communication.

COURSEWRITER   A computer assisted instruction author language produced by IBM for large computers. The language was produced in three successive versions over time: COURSEWRITER, COURSEWRITER II, and COURSEWRITER III. This language is significant because it was the model upon which many other manufacturer's CAI author languages were based.

Credibility   Learners have an easier time learning material and recalling it later if they have respect for the source of the material. You may find that it strengthens your lessons if in some cases you provide the students with information about the credibility of the source.

Criterion frames   Criterion frames are special purpose frames which function to test the student's attainment of criterion levels of learning. Their main characteristic that enables them to function as such, is their freedom from prompting — this ensures that only students who have mastered the content represented can answer the frames correctly. Some CAI authors use criterion frames in place of objectives.

Crowderian lesson design   Any CAI lesson design which uses the principles developed by Norman Crowder. Also called an intrinsic or scrambled lesson design.

Cue   Additional information provided to a student to increase the likelihood that he or she will get the correct response. The term **prompt,** which is more often used, is synonymous. **Hint** is another, similar term which is often used to mean approximately the same thing.

Default value   When a program provides the student with options and the student fails to choose an option, the program is usually set up to choose for the student.

The option the program chooses is called, technically, the default value.

Discovery learning   A lesson design strategy in which the conditions are provided within which the student can "discover" basic principles, or relationships, rather than have them presented explicitly. The assumption is that students will develop superior understanding and better retention by being required to exercise their reason in this manner.

Discrimination   The act of recognizing differences among a set of somewhat similar things. It usually refers to frame styles or to lesson designs in which the student is expected to learn to tell the difference between things.

Discrimination stimulus   The specific feature or characteristic of a thing that is sufficient to differentiate it from another thing which is otherwise the same.

Distractor   In an alternative response frame, the term **distractor** refers to the incorrect alternatives provided to "distract" the student from the correct response(s).

Distribution of emphasis   This is an important concept in all pedagogical endeavors. It refers to the amount of instructional time, space, resources, examples, and other reinforcing techniques that are applied to each item to be learned. Ideally, the most emphasis will be given to those items which intuition and experience indicate are likely to be the most difficult for the student to learn. Unfortunately, the reverse is often the case.

Divergent questioning   The use of questions specifically designed to widen the frame of reference of a lesson.

Documentation   Written, descriptive material and instructions which accompany and facilitate the use of computer software, courseware, and programs.

EGRUL   An acronym which stands for example (**EG**) and rule (**RUL**). It refers to the design of a lesson in which the student is given examples, cases, or other specific items and is then expected to deduce a rule, law, principle, or other general characteristic.

Emphasis   A technique used to strengthen a lesson. It might consist of redundancy, recasting, use of examples, hyperbole, metaphor, analogy, or any technique that makes the lesson easier to learn, or makes the material easier to remember.

Enabling objectives   Objectives whose value is only temporary, during the course of the lesson. Enabling objectives are so called because they involve learning tasks which enable the student to accomplish the more important, terminal objectives. The terminal objectives, by contradistinction, refer to those objectives which result in more or less permanent changes in the student's abilities.

Entering behaviors   Those skills and abilities which students are assumed to bring to the learning situation. Also referred to as prerequisite skills.

Entrance behaviors   (**See** Entering behaviors.)

Entry level skills   (**See** Entering behaviors.)

Error   Technical term for a student's incorrect responses.

Error rate   The ratio of correct responses to incorrect responses, usually expressed as the percentage of incorrect responses or errors.

191

Exemplar   A technical term for an example, usually of a class of things to be learned or discriminated from the members of another class. In concept learning, any one of members which illustrate the concept.

Exit criteria   The level of performance which a student must demonstrate before leaving a lesson or section of a lesson.

Extrinsic motivation   Incentives for performance which come from outside the immediate situation, or are not an intrinsic part of the situation.

Extrinsic program   Theoretically an extrinsic program is any program which requires that the student supply as a response, material which is not found at that point in the program or perhaps is not found in the program at all — or, is "extrinsic" to the program. Any program which is in contradistinction to an "intrinsic program."

Facilitation of learning   Any process which makes learning easier or more likely to occur.

Fading   A lesson design in which the prompts are gradually removed so that responses are increasingly based on the student's recall. A particularly useful technique for the memorization of material such as anatomy charts or poetry.

Feedback   The flow of information about the outcome of an action back to the source of the action so that it may be used to improve subsequent actions. Synonymous with **knowledge of results** for instructional systems design purposes.

Foil   Any of the alternatives in an alternative choice frame.

Forced choice   A characteristic of an alternative choice frame in which the student is required to select one of the choices provided; the student is not permitted the option of indicating that none of the alternative choices provided is correct.

Formal prompt   A prompt is any assistance provided within the CAI lesson which increases the likelihood that a student will make the correct response. A **formal** prompt is one which uses the structure, or "form" of the frame to do this, rather than using the theme of the material as a thematic prompt does.

Format   The structure or layout of material such as a frame or a CAI lesson. With computers it can also refer to the preparation of a disk to receive data.

Frame   In CAI, the term **frame** refers to the amount of material that appears on the viewing screen at any one time.

Generalization   Having learned all the features or characteristics of one exemplar, the student may be expected to identify a subset of the features in other exemplars. Such learning or exercise is referred to as generalization.

Heuristic   A kind of algorithm which is capable of changing itself based on its own performance record.

Higher-order question   There have been several hierarchies of human thought processes developed. In all of them there is the assumption that the higher the level, the more sophisticated the thought process involved. Higher-order questions are those which require the student to use thought processes which represent the upper levels of the hierarchies. The importance of this concept for CAI authors is that the level of thought process involved in the learning process should be matched to the learning outcomes desired. It is wasteful of student time and effort to teach at a higher level than the outcome requires. Similarly, it is unfair to the student to teach at too low a level and then either test or otherwise require student performance at a higher level.

Highlighting   A process which causes some of the characters on the computer display screen to stand out. Typically, it involves causing some characters to be lighted with a greater intensity or level of brightness than others. Only some microcomputers have this capacity.

Hint   Usually refers to a delayed attempt to assist the student in obtaining the correct answer by supplying additional information or calling attention to certain parts of the information he or she already has. Usually it is done verbally, after the student has either hesitated a long time or has made an incorrect response.

Hyperbole   Calling attention to the most outstanding member of a class of things. Also, it may be the exaggeration of a characteristic, for didactic purposes.

Initial behavior   (**See** Entering behaviors)

Instructional moves   A technical term which applies to any action taken by an instructor (or instructional system) to change the direction, or the course, of instruction. An instructional move may, for example, broaden or narrow a frame of reference. It may also be used to postpone an activity until later in the instructional sequence.

Instructional systems design   A generic term for the procedures involved in constructing learning activities which comprise a solution to a complex set of learning problems. Any type of media or learning approach may be employed so long as the principles and techniques generally accepted to be part of the "systems approach" are used. The approach typically involves

1. Written documentation specifying learning outcomes.

2. Selection and creation of learning activities to match and accomplish learning outcomes.

3. Utilization of feedback to improve the learning activities.

Interactive   A term which describes a learning process in which the student and the system alternate in addressing each other. Typically, each is capable of selecting alternative actions based on the actions of the other.

Intrinsic motivation   Motivation which arises from the doing of the thing itself, rather than from the anticipation of some additional reward or payoff from outside (extrinsic to) the learning environment.

Intrinsic Program   Refers, conventionally, to a very specific type of program in which students are offered response alternatives. Then, depending upon which response alternative they choose, they are directed to a different part of the program at which point they are informed as to the appropriateness of their response. Intrinsic programs are also referred to as **branching texts, scrambled texts,** or **Crowderian Programs** (the latter after Norman Crowder, a pioneering programmer credited with having originated this technique). Intrinsic programs are often contrasted with extrinsic, or linear, programs as mutually exclusive categories.

ISD   Instructional systems design.

Joy stick   A type of control or input device for a microcomputer, consisting of a short vertical lever which can be moved in any direction. The position of the joy stick is then transmitted to the microcomputer, where it may be used to control the position of the cursor or perhaps some graphic figure. This can be a useful feature in CAI intended for children or others who cannot use the keyboard to make inputs.

Knowledge of results   Feedback provided to a
student with respect to performance in a CAI lesson. In
any systems application, it is the information fed back
to an origin of an effect that is used to improve
subsequent performance at that site.

Law of Effect   The Law of Effect is the primary
principle of behavior upon which operant conditioning,
and indeed behavioral psychology, is based. It is also
the main principle upon which programmed instruction, and
CAI, is based. Briefly stated, it says that behavior
which is followed by pleasant consequences is more likely
to be repeated than behavior which is not. The
assumption is that it is pleasant to find out that your
response is correct, and therefore you will tend to make
that response again when faced with the same situation.

Light pen   An attachment for a microcomputer which
allows the student to indicate a point on the screen
merely by touching the light pen to that point. The
computer has both the hardware and the software
capability to sense exactly where the light pen is
pointed on the screen.

Linear Program   A program which contains little or
no branching. In other words, every student who goes
through the lesson sees exactly the same information and
questions. The logical branching which occurs in
providing feedback to either a correct response or an
incorrect response does not disqualify a lesson as
linear.

Matching items   Alternative response question
frames in which the student is asked to indicate which
items from one list go with or "match" which items from a
second list.

Menu   A set of instructions for running a program
which are built in to the program so that they appear on
the screen, allowing the user to merely select options
rather than remember them. They are a great convenience,
and often eliminate the need for additional, written
instructions on paper. Menus are one of the features
which are referred to when people speak of a
microcomputer as "friendly."

Menu-driven   Refers to a program, the running of which is controlled by a menu.

Metaphor   Referring to an entity as if it were another entity, or ascribing to something capabilities or characteristics it does not have, is using metaphor. The metaphor is one of the most useful teaching devices. It allows us to speak of the thing to be learned as if it was something students were already familiar with.

Mnemonic device   Any device which can be used as a memory aid to make something easier to remember.

Multiple-choice frame   An alternative response frame style in which the student is provided with a number of foils from which to choose the correct response.

Negative transfer of learning   When learning one thing interferes with the learning of something else, it is said to produce negative transfer.

Overcuing   When a frame has so many cues or prompts that it is difficult to tell why the student responded correctly, it is said to be overcued.

Panel   Usually refers to a graphic display, such as a table or mechanical drawing, which accompanies a lesson for the student's reference.

Positive reinforcement   In operationalizing the Law of Effect, it is common to provide for pleasant consequence to follow the performance of an act which we wish to have repeated. In practical terms, for CAI it means providing prompt, supportive feedback when the student makes a correct response, under the assumption that finding out that your answer is correct constitutes positive reinforcement.

Positive transfer of learning   When the learning of one thing makes it easier to learn something else, positive transfer of learning is said to have occurred.

Prerequisite   Usually refers to the prior learning upon which the current lesson depends.

Proactive inhibition   A technical term referring to the concept that something which has been learned earlier can interfere with the learning of a later lesson. Distinguished from retroactive inhibition in which later learning interferes with the retention of something which was learned earlier.

Programmed instruction   Any instructional materials which use the principles of programmed instruction:

   1. Small steps

   2. Active responding

   3. Prompt feedback

Programmed versus programed   There are two, contradictory spelling rules which govern the spelling of this term. One says that when a word ends in a consonant, one doubles the final consonant and adds **ed** to form the past tense. The other rule says that when the accent is on the last syllable, it is not necessary to double the final consonant when forming the past tense of the word. One sees it done both ways but in the programmed instruction field, **programed** seems to be more popular. It should be obvious which this author prefers.

Prompt   Any technique which is built in to the lesson to help the student make the correct response. (**See** Formal prompt and Thematic prompt.

Protocol   An example of a class of items, such as CAI frames, which is so typical of its kind that it can be used as a model for the creation of new items.

Question frame   Any CAI frame in which the student is expected to make a response.

Recasting   Rewriting or rewording a frame so that the student has an opportunity to make additional associations and increase the likelihood of learning and making a correct response.

Redundancy   Repeating a word, term, or longer passage verbatim, so as to increase the likelihood of retention. Similar to recasting but does not include rewording.

Reinforce   To increase the likelihood that a given response will be repeated if the student is faced with the same frame.

Reinforcement   Any device, technique, or action which serves to increase the likelihood that a given response will be made again, given functionally similar circumstances. Most instructional programmers regard the feedback given to a student to confirm a correct response as reinforcement for that response.

Response   Usually refers to the product of the student's response rather than the response itself since it is the product or consequence of the response that is recorded by the computer, that is, the constructed answer or an indication of choice among a set of alternatives. The response can either be a response which is constructed by the student, or it can be the student's indicated choice among a set of alternative response options provided for him or her to choose from.

Response economy   Response economy refers to the relative amount of time and effort which the student must expend in order to provide an answer or response to a question. Unless there is a valid and compelling pedagogical reason to do otherwise, the most economic response mode possible should be chosen. The CAI author has a responsibility to present the student with the most favorable possible "pain-to-gain ratio," or effort-to-learning-progress ratio.

Response generalization   A technical term referring to the student's learned ability to recognize when the same response can be made to alternative questions.

Response latency   Response latency refers to the time elapsed from the student's earliest opportunity to make a response until he or she finally does. There are several practical implications of this for CAI authors. During the validation process, the CAI author should endeavor to reduce the length of response latencies by improving frames.
  Response latency can also be used as a criterion for judging student performance. The longer the latency, the greater the probability that the student will make an incorrect response; or at least the greater the probability that he or she lacks confidence and could benefit from a remedial loop. One useful technique, in systems that will permit it, is to keep track of student latency and interrupt the student to provide clues, more instruction, or an alternative question frame.

Response mode   The manner in which the student is expected to make a response to a question frame. The two main types are alternative responses, in which the student is expected to choose an alternative from among two or more options provided, and constructed responses, in which the student is expected to create an answer or response to a question frame. The term is occasionally extended to refer to response modes such as written, spoken, or demonstrated response.

Response shaping   Occasionally a student is required to learn to make a response which is extremely complicated, and beyond his or her initial ability. A common technique in such a case is to accept simplified forms of the response early in the lesson, and then gradually require more and more sophisticated forms of the response throughout the lesson until the final sophisticated form of the response is obtained. Such a technique is referred to as response shaping.

Retention   A technical term for remembering. Retention is often referred to as a percentage of the original amount learned which is recalled on a post-test. Retention is usually plotted over time, or the number of times recall is attempted. In CAI, as a practical matter, it is often an all or nothing affair with respect to a specific item to be learned.

Retroactive inhibition   The extent to which something learned later interferes with the retention of something which was learned earlier. A good example of this is people who learn to drive a car with a clutch, then spends some time driving a car with an automatic transmission, and then find that they have trouble when they go back to the car with the clutch.

RULEG   An acronym for a frame type or lesson design which proceeds from rule(RUL) to example(EG).

S   The shorthand which behavioral psychologists use for **stimulus** in the stimulus(S)-response(R)-reinforcement(r) model.

S d   In multiple-choice frames, the correct responses are referred to technically as S d's.

S delta   In multiple choice frames, the incorrect choices are referred to technically as S deltas.

Schedule of reinforcement   In operant conditioning experiments, it is common to test different patterns of providing and withholding reinforcement. In other words, not every correct response needs to be reinforced. In fact, some patterns of reinforcement (tecnically, schedules of reinforcement) produce learning which is more resistant to forgetting than do others.

Scope   The scope of a lesson refers to its size, or the amount of content covered.

Scrambled program   A term used to refer to a particular style of programmed text in which the student is asked an alternative response question at the end of each page (approximately). Depending on the answer selected, the student is directed to a different page in the book. The technique has not been exploited on computers, but could probably be adapted quite nicely to CAI applications for certain materials.

Scrambled text   (**See** Scrambled program)

Screen   The exposed face of the cathode ray tube, used as a display on most terminals and microcomputers.

Scroll   The manner in which text is sometimes moved on a CRT screen. Specifically, the text on the screen moves either up or down the screen continuously, usually with each new line of text occurring at one end of the screen simultaneously with the disappearance from the screen of the oldest line of text.

Self-paced   Any instructional presentation technique in which the pace of the lesson is adjusted to fit the requirements of the individual student. Technically, it should refer only to those lessons in which the student is in complete control of the rate at which the lesson is accomplished.

Sequence   The order in which the materials in a lesson are arranged. Often, the scope and sequence are considered together as a lesson is planned.

Serial learning   A special class of learning in which a list of steps, concepts, or other items must be learned in a specific, exact sequence.

Simulation   Simulation is the generic name given to a type of program which embodies a model that is analogous to some real system, and which permits variables to be changed in such a way as to reveal the operation of the system. Simulations are an important class of learning tools which are, in a broad sense, CAI.

Skinnerian program   A term occasionally used to refer to a linear lesson design which stereotypically illustrates behavioral principles and techniques.

SMS   An abbreviation for subject matter specialist.

Socratic method   A method of instruction in which learning proceeds entirely or predominantly from the teacher or the instructional system asking questions of the student.

Stem   The main part, or first part, of a multiple choice question frame; everything but the foils.

Step size   The amount of new material covered by each frame.

Stimulus   In the behavioral model, the stimulus is the condition to which the subject must respond. In CAI, it is the question frame.

Strand   The **strand** is a term sometimes used to identify one parallel element, or track, of a complex curriculum.

Strategy I   A developmental-validation strategy in which only the criterion frames are written prior to the first cycle of validation. Each additional change to the lesson is then based strictly on empirical validation data.

Strategy II   A developmental-validation strategy in which the author prepares a very lean version of the lesson, anticipating the addition of lesson material in response to the need indicated by empirical validation data.

Strategy III   A developmental-validation strategy in which the author prepares a lesson which he or she considers to be complete. The author is aware that no validation is likely to take place.

Structured program   Any program in which the structure of the program is determined by a strict hierarchical relationship. PASCAL is considered to be a structured programming language.

Structuring move   Any instructional strategy which is intended to narrow the field of consideration or introduce a more precise form to the direction or course of a didactic event.

Subject matter specialist   A content expert used as a consultant in an instructional-systems-design effort to ensure the accuracy of factual material in a lesson.

Successive approximation   The process of guiding a student's responses toward a more and more acceptable form.

Syllogism   A form of logical argument that is particularly useful in instructional designs and in the logic of question frame construction.

Tactile   A surface or instrument which is reactive to touch. A tactile terminal is one which can sense the fact that a student is touching a specific portion of the screen.

Task analysis   The process of examining or studying the smallest unit of work in a job role, or the smallest transaction in a learning situation.

Task analysis by selected criteria   A specific method of task analysis in which the tasks are analyzed in terms of a set of specific variables or characteristics.

Task simulator   In a learning system it is sometimes necessary to require the student to approximate a task by means of a specially constructed device which produces an artificial semblance of the conditions under which the task must ultimately be performed.

Tasky   When a learning situation involves a lot of physical work on the part of the student, it is said to be tasky.

Terminal behaviors   The new skills, knowledge, and abilities that students have at the completion of a lesson that they did not have at the beginning of the lesson constitute terminal behaviors.

Terminal performance   The demonstration of terminal behaviors.

Terminal response   The last response in a lesson sequence which deals with a single topic. Usually used to refer to the response required in a sequence which involves a progression toward a more sophisticated response, such as a shaping sequence or a fading sequence.

Thematic prompt   A cue (prompt) built in to the lesson, the utility of which depends upon a comprehension of the content (theme) of the lesson.

Top-down design   A programming concept in which the structure of the program follows a strict pattern of hierarchical subordination. The virtue of such a program lies in the ease with which the program can be understood, and the program can be modified, even by people other than the original programmer.

Tracking   A term used to refer to the way in which a program will follow a correct line of logic and not get stalled in an endless loop or some other nonfunctional condition. In a multitrack lesson design the parallel lines of lesson options are called tracks; thus, following one of them correctly is called tracking.

Transfer of learning   Transfer of learning is said to occur when the learning of one thing affects, either positively or negatively, the learning or retention of another thing.

Try-out   A term sometimes used to refer to the field-test phase of validation.

Validated instruction   Any instructional system which has undergone a conscientious validation process of testing and revision.

Validation   The process of field testing materials and revising them on the basis of field test data.

Validation data   The statistical evidence of the validation process.

Verbal learning   Any learning task which is primarily verbal, and which is intended to produce verbal skills.

INDEX